1 MONTH OF
FREE
READING

at

www.ForgottenBooks.com

By purchasing this book you are eligible for one month membership to ForgottenBooks.com, giving you unlimited access to our entire collection of over 1,000,000 titles via our web site and mobile apps.

To claim your free month visit:

www.forgottenbooks.com/free218728

ISBN 978-0-483-97728-0
PIBN 10218728

ELIAS HICKS

FROM BUST BY PARTRIDGE

THE LIFE AND LABORS

OF

ELIAS HICKS

BY

Henry W. Wilbur

Introduction by
ELIZABETH POWELL BOND

~~~~~

PHILADELPHIA
Published by Friends' General Conference Advancement Committee
1910

CONTENTS.

LIST OF ILLUSTRATIONS.

AUTHOR'S PREFACE.

Elias Hicks was a much misunderstood man in his own time, and the lapse of eighty years since his death has done but little to make him known to the passing generations. His warm personal friends, and of them there were many, considered him little less than a saint; his enemies, some of whom were intensely bitter in their personal feeling, whatever may have been the basis of their judgment, believed him to be a man whose influence was malevolent and mischievous. It is no part of the purpose of this book to attempt to reconcile the conflicting estimates touching the life and character of this remarkable man. On the contrary, our hope is to present him as he was, in his own environment, and not at all as he might have been had he lived in our time, or as his admirers would have him, to make him conform to their own estimate. In this biographical task, Elias Hicks becomes largely his own interpreter. As he measured himself in private correspondence and in public utterance, so this book will endeavor to measure him.

We believe that it is not too much to say that he carried the fundamental idea of the Society of Friends, as delivered by George Fox, to its logical conclusion, as applied to thought and life, more clearly and forcibly than any of his predecessors or contemporaries. Not a few of those who violently opposed him, discounted the position of Fox and Barclay touching the Inner Light, and gave exaggerated importance to the claims of evangelical theology. Whatever others may have thought, Elias Hicks believed that he preached Christianity of the pure apostolic type, and

Quakerism as it was delivered by the founders. It should be remembered that the conformist and non-conformist disputants of the seventeenth century talked as savagely about Fox as the early nineteenth century critics did about Hicks. In fact, to accept the theory of Fox about the nature and office of the indwelling spirit, necessarily develops either indifference or opposition to the plans and theories of what was in the time of Elias Hicks, if it is not now, the popularly accepted theology.

No attempt has been made to write a comprehensive and detailed history of the so-called "separation." So far, however, as the trouble related to Elias Hicks, it has been considered, and as much light as possible has been thrown on the case. Necessarily this does not admit of very much reference to the setting up of separate meetings, which followed the open rupture of 1827-28, or the contests over property which occurred after the death of Elias Hicks. Even the causes of the trouble in the Society only appear as they seem necessary to make plain the feeling of Elias Hicks in the case, and the attitude of his opponents toward him.

In dealing with the doctrines of Elias Hicks, or his views about various subjects, we have endeavored to avoid the one-sided policy, and to discriminate between the matters which would be accepted by the majority of those Friends to-day who are erroneously made to bear the name of Elias Hicks, and the theories which they now repudiate. On the other hand, his most conservative and peculiar ideas are given equal prominence with those which more nearly conform to present-day thought.

In stating cases of antagonism, especially where it appeared in public meetings, we have endeavored rather to give samples, than to repeat and amplify occurrences where the same purpose and spirit were exhibited. The citations in the book should, therefore, be taken as types, and not as mere isolated or extraordinary occurrences.

References to the descendants of Elias Hicks, and other matters relating to his life, which do not seem to naturally belong in the coherent and detailed story, will be found in the appendix. This is also true of the usual acknowledgment of assistance, and the reference to the published sources of information consulted by the author in writing the book.

2

INTRODUCTION.

Now and again a human life is lived in such obedience to the "heavenly vision" that it becomes an authority in other lives. The unswerving rectitude; whence is its divine directness? the world has to ask. Its clear-sightedness; how comes it that the eye is single to the true course? Its strength to endure; from what fountain flows unfailing strength? Its quickening sympathy; what is the sweet secret?

The thought of the world fixes itself into stereotyped and imprisoning forms from which only the white heat of the impassioned seer and prophet can slowly liberate it. At last the world ceases to persecute or to crucify its liberator, and lo! an acknowledged revelation of God! This came to pass in the seventeenth century, when it was given George Fox to see and to proclaim that "there was an anointing within man to teach him, and that the Lord would teach him, himself."

The eighteenth century developed another teacher in the religious society of Friends, whose message has been a distinctly leavening influence in the thought of the world. It is not easy to account for Elias Hicks. He was not the "son of a prophet." Nor was he a gift from the *schools* of the time in which he lived. In the "Journal of His Life and Religious Labours," published in 1832 by Isaac T. Hopper, there is no reference to school days.

There is one clue to this man that may explain much to us. Of his ancestry he says in the restrained language characteristic of his writings, "My parents were descended from reputable families, and sustained a good character along their friends and those who knew them." Here, then, is the rock-foundation upon which he builded, the factor which could not be spared from the life which he lived—that in his veins was the blood of those who had "sustained a good character among those who knew them." Some of the leisure of his youth had been given to fishing and fowling, which he looked back to as wholesome recreation, since he mostly preferred going alone. While he waited in stillness for the coming of the fowl, his mind was at times so taken up in divine meditations, that the opportunities were seasons of instruction and comfort to him.' Out of these meditations grew the conviction in his tendered soul that it was wanton diversion for himself and his companions to destroy the small birds that could be of no use to them.

Recalling his youth, he writes: "Some of my leisure hours were occupied in reading the Scriptures, in which I took considerable delight, and it tended to my real profit and religious improvement." It may be that this great classic in English, as well as library of ancient history, and book of spiritual revelation, was not only the food that stimulated his spiritual growth, but also took the place to him, in some measure, of the schools as a means of culture. It is plain to see that he had what is the first requisite for a student—a hungering mind. The alphabet opened to him the ways and means, which he used as far as he could, for the satisfying of this divine hunger. A new book possessed for him such charm, it is said, that his friends who invited him for a social visit, knowing this, were careful to put the new books out of sight, lest he should become absorbed in them, and they lose his ever-welcome and very entertaining conversation. He even had experience as a teacher; and the testimony is given by an aged Friend, once his pupil: "The manners of Elias Hicks were so mild, his deportment so dignified, and his conversation so instructive, that it left an impression for good on many of his pupils' minds that time never effaced."

That he had not the teaching of the schools narrowed his own resources, and, doubtless, restricted his field of vision. But such a life as his, that garnered wisdom more than knowledge of books, is a great encouragement to those who have not had the opportunities of the schools. We might not know without being told that he had missed from his equipment a college degree; but we do know that his endowment of sound mind was supplemented with incorruptible character; we do know that his life was founded upon belief in everlasting truth and an unchanging integrity. The record of his unfolding spiritual life shows that

> "So nigh is grandeur to our dust,
> So near is God to man,
> When Duty whispers low, 'Thou must,'
> The youth replies, 'I can.' "

There is evidence that Elias Hicks had not only a hungering mind, but that he had in marked degree the open mind, and that he accorded to others liberty of opinion. It is said that he was unwilling that his discourses be printed, lest they become a bondage to other minds. He wrote to his friend, William Poole: "Therefore every generation must have more light than the preceding one; otherwise, they must sit down in ease in the labour and works of their predecessors." And he left a word of caution to approaching age, when he said in a meeting in New York: "The old folks think they have got far enough, they are settling on the lees, they are blocking up the way." It does not disturb my thought of him that my own mother remembered a mild rebuke from him for the modest flower-bed that brightened the door-yard of her country home. For I discover in him rudiments of the love for beauty. A minister among Friends was once his guest during the harvest season on Long Island, and recalled long after that, when the hour arrived for the mid-week meeting, he came in from the harvest field, and not only exchanged his working for his meeting garments, but added his gloves, although it was not, midsummer weather. There was certainly the rudimentary love for beauty in this scrupulous regard for the proprieties; but it was kept in such severe check that he could not justify the spending of time upon a flower-border. The poet had not then expressed for us the sweet garden prayer that might have brought to his sensitive mind a new view of the purpose and value of the flower-border:

> "That we were earthlings and of earth must live,
> Thou knowest, Allah, and did'st give us bread;
> Yea, and remembering of our souls, didst give
> Us food of flowers; thy name be hallowed!"

From the days in which he preferred his hours of solitude in fishing as opportunities for "divine meditations" we can trace his steady spiritual growth. While his business life was henceforth subordinated to his labors among men to promote the life of the spirit, he was never indifferent to the exact discharge of his own financial obligations; nor was he indifferent to the needs of others. One incident surely marks him as belonging to the School of Christ: "Once when harvests were light and provisions scarce and high, his own wheat fields yielded abundantly. Foreseeing the scarcity and consequent rise in prices, speculators sought early to buy his wheat. He declined to sell. They offered him large prices, and renewed their visits repeatedly, increasing the price each time. Still he refused to sell, even for the unprecedented sum of three dollars a bushel. But by and by, when his poorer neighbors, whose crops were light, began to need, he invited them to come and get as much wheat as they required for use, at the usual price of one dollar a bushel."

He entered into the life of his community and of his times, anticipating by nearly a century the work of Friends' Philanthropic Committees of the present day. It is related that he was much opposed to an attempt to establish a liquor-selling tavern in the Jericho neighborhood—that when he saw strangers approaching he would invite them to accept his own hospitality, thus making unnecessary the tavern-keeping business in the sparsely settled country town.

We would expect that, with his sense of justice and his appreciation of values, Elias Hicks would place men and women side by side, not only in the home, but also in the larger household of faith, and in the affairs of the world. It is remembered that his face was set in this direction—that, strict Society-disciplinarian as he was, he advocated a change in the Discipline to allow women a consulting voice in making and amending the Discipline.

It must be borne in mind that he lived through the Revolutionary period of 1776, and through the War of 1812. So true was he to his convictions against war that he would not allow himself to benefit by the advanced prices in foodstuffs; and we are told that the records of his monthly meeting show that he sacrificed much of his property by adherence to his peace principles.

Neither can we forget the testing that came to him in the institution of slavery. For, according to the custom of the times, his own father was the owner of slaves. His open mind responded to the labors of a committee of the New York Yearly Meeting; and upon the freeing of his father's slaves, he ever after considered their welfare, making such restitution as he could for past injustice.

To his daughter, Martha Hicks, he wrote: "My dear love to thee, to thy dear mother, who next to the Divine Blesser has been the joy of thy youth, and who, I trust and hope, will be the comfort of thy declining years. O dear child, cherish and help her, for she hath done abundance for thee."

These fruits of the religious faith of Elias Hicks are offered as the test given us by the Great Teacher himself, by which to know the life of a man. They mark a life rooted in the life of God. Imperishable as the root whence they grew, may they feed the souls of men from generation to generation, satisfying the hungry, strengthening the weak, and making all glad in the joy of each! Thus it is permitted to be "still praising Him."

ELIZABETH POWELL BOND.

CHAPTER I.

Ancestry and Boyhood.

THE Hicks family is English in its origin, authentic history tracing it clearly back to the fourteenth century. By a sort of genealogical paradox, a far-away ancestor of the apostle of peace in the eighteenth century was a man of war, for we are told that Sir Ellis Hicks was knighted on the battlefield of Poitiers in 1356, nearly four hundred years before the birth of his distinguished descendant on Long Island, in America.

From the best available data, it is believed that the progenitor of the Hicks family on Long Island arrived in America in 1638, and came over from the New England mainland about 1645, settling in the town of Hempstead. A relative, Robert by name, came over with the body of Pilgrims arriving in Massachusetts in 1621.

John Hicks, the pioneer, was undoubtedly a man of affairs, with that strong character which qualifies men for leadership. In the concerns of the new community he was often drafted for important public service. In Seventh month, 1647, it became necessary to reach a final settlement with the Indians for land purchased from them by the colonists the year before. The adjustment of this transaction was committed to John Hicks by his neighbors. When, in 1663, the English towns on the island and the New York mainland created a council whose aim it was to secure aid from the General Court at Hartford against the Dutch, John Hicks was made a delegate from Long Island. In 1665 Governor Nicoll, of New York, called a convention

17

to be composed of two delegates from each town in West-chester County and on Long Island, "to make additions and alterations to existing laws." John Hicks was chosen delegate from the town of Hempstead.

Thomas, the great grandfather of Elias, was in 1691 appointed the first judge of Queens County, by Governor Andross, which office he held for a number of years, with credit to himself and satisfaction to his constituents.

The town of Hempstead is on the north side of Long Island, and borders on the Sound. There Elias Hicks, the fifth in line of descent from the pioneer John, was born on the 19th of Third month, 1748. He was the fourth child of John and Martha Smith Hicks. Of the ancestry of the mother of Elias little is known. There is no evidence that the ancestors of Elias on either side were members of the Society of Friends, still they seem to have had much in common with Friends, and, at any rate, were willing to assist the peculiar people when the heavy hand of persecution fell upon them. In this connection we may quote the words of Elias himself. He says: "My father was a grandson of Thomas Hicks, of whom our worthy friend Samuel Bownas[2] makes honorable mention in his Journal, and by whom he was much comforted and

---

[2] Samuel Bownas was a minister among Friends, and was born in Westmoreland, England, about 1667. He secured a minute to make a religious visit to America the latter part of 1701. Ninth month 30, 1702, he was bound over to the Queens County Grand Jury, the charge against him being that in a sermon he had spoken disparagingly of the Church of England. The jury really failed to indict him, which greatly exasperated the presiding judge, who threatened to deport him to London chained to the man-of-war's deck. It was at this point that Thomas Hicks, whom Bownas erroneously concluded was Chief Justice of the Province, appeared to comfort and assure him that he could not thus be deported to England. Bownas continued in jail for about a year, during which time he learned the shoemaker's trade. He was finally liberated by proclamation.

strengthened when imprisoned through the envy of George Keith,[3] at Jamaica, on Long Island."[4]

We are told in the Journal, "Neither of my parents were members in strict fellowship with any religious society, until some little time before my birth."[5] It is certain that the father of Elias was a member along Friends at the time of his birth, and his mother must also have enjoyed such membership. Elias must have been a birthright member, as he nowhere mentions having been received into the Society by convincement. It is evident that his older brothers and sisters were not connected with Friends.

When Elias was eight years of age his father removed from Hempstead to the south shore of Long Island, the new home being near the seashore. Both before and after that time he bewails the fact that his associates were not Friends, and what he confessed was worse—they were persons with no religious inclinations or connections whatever.

The new home afforded added opportunities for pleasure. Game was plentiful in the wild fowl that mated in the marshes and meadows, while the bays and inlets abounded in fish. Hunting and fishing, therefore, became his principal diversion. While he severely condemned this form of amusement in later life, he brought to the whole matter a rational philosophy. He considered that at the

---

[3] George Keith, born near Aberdeen, 1639, became connected with the Society of Friends about 1662. He came to America in 1684, but finally separated from Friends, and endeavored to organize a new sect to be called Christian, or Baptist Quakers. This effort failed, and about 1700 he entered the Church of England. After this he violently criticised Friends, and repeatedly sought controversy with them. He had quite an experience of this sort with Samuel Bownas, and was considered the real instigator of the complaint on which Bownas was lodged in jail. Keith looms up large in all that body of history and biography unfriendly to the Society of Friends.

[4] Journal of Elias Hicks, p. 7.

[5] Journal of Elias Hicks, p. 7.

time hunting and fishing were profitable to him, because in his exposed condition "they had a tendency to keep me more at and about home, and often prevented my joining with loose company, which I had frequent opportunities of doing without my father's knowledge."

Three years after moving to the new home, when Elias was eleven years of age, his mother was removed by death. The father, thus left with six children, two younger than Elias, finally found it necessary to divide the family. Two years after the death of his mother he went to reside with one of his elder brothers who was married, and lived some distance from his father's. It is probable that this brother's house was his home most of the time until he was seventeen. Much regret is expressed by him that he was thus removed from parental restraint.

The Journal makes possibly unnecessarily sad confession of what he considered waywardness during this period. He says that he wandered far from "the salutary path of true religion, learning to sing vain songs, and to take delight in running horses." [6] Just what the songs were, and the exact character of the horse racing must be mainly a matter of conjecture. Manifestly "running horses" did not mean at all the type of racetrack gambling with which twentieth-century Long Island is familiar.

In the midst of self-accusation, he declares that he did not "give way to anything which was commonly accounted disreputable, having always a regard to strict honesty, and to such a line of conduct as comported with politeness and good breeding." [7] One can scarcely think of Elias Hicks as a juvenile Chesterfield. From the most unfavorable things he says about himself, the conclusion is easily reached that he was really a serious-minded youth, and what has

---

[6] Journal of Elias Hicks, p. 8.

[7] Journal, p. 8.

always been considered a "good boy." It must be remembered, however, that he set for himself a high standard, which was often violated, as he became what he called "hardened in vanity." Speaking of his youthful sports, and possible waywardness, his maturer judgment confessed, that but "for the providential care of my Heavenly Father, my life would have fallen a sacrifice to my folly and indiscretion." [3]

There is practically no reference to the matter of schools or schooling in the Journal. There is every reason for the belief that he was self-educated. He may have had a brief experience at schools of a rather primary character. At all events he must have had a considerable acquaintance with mathematics, and evidently he at an early age contracted the reading habit. Books were few, and of periodical literature there was none. Friendly literature itself was confined to Sewell's History, probably Ellwood's edition of George Fox's Journal, while he may have had access to some of the controversial pamphlets of the seventeenth century period. The Journals of various "ancient" Friends were to be had, but how rich the mine of this literature which he explored we shall never know. Evidently from his youth he was a careful and intelligent reader of the Bible, and regarding its passages, its ethics and its theology, he became his own interpreter.

---

[3] Journal of Elias Hicks, p. 9.

CHAPTER II

His Young Manhood.

AT THE age of seventeen Elias became an apprentice, and set about learning the carpenter's trade. His mechanical experience during this period receives practically no attention in the Journal. We know, however, that in those days none of the trades were divided into sectional parts as now. In short, he learned a whole trade, and not part of one. It was the day of hand-made doors, and not a few carpenters took the timber standing in the forest, and superintended or personally carried on all of the processes of transforming it into lumber and from it producing the finished product. The carpenter of a century and a half ago had to be able to wield the broad-ax, and literally know how to "hew to the line."

It is not known exactly how long this apprenticeship lasted, but probably about four years. As a matter of course, there was much moving from neighborhood to neighborhood, as the building necessities demanded the presence of the carpenters. The life was more or less irregular, and Elias says that he received neither serious advice nor restraint at the hands of his "master." He was brought in contact with frivolously minded young people, and was unduly carried away with the love of amusement. During this period he learned to dance, and enjoyed the experience. But he considered dancing a most mischievous pastime, and evil to a marked degree. For this indulgence he repeatedly upbraided himself in the Journal. In his opinion, dancing was "an unnatural and unchristian practice," never receiving the approval "of the divine light in the secret of the heart."

He passed through various experiences in the endeavor to break away from the dancing habit, with many backslidings, overthrowing what he considered his good resolutions. But finally he separated from all those companions of his youth who beset him with temptation. He says: "I was deeply tried, but the Lord was graciously near; and as my cry was secretly to him for strength, he enabled me to covenant with him, that if he would be pleased in mercy to empower me, I would forever cease from this vain and sinful amusement." [1]

His first initiation touching the eternally lost condition of the wicked is in connection with his experience at this time. We cannot do better than to quote his own words:

"In looking back to this season of deep probation, my soul has been deeply humbled; for I had cause to believe that if I had withstood at this time the merciful interposition of divine love, and had rebelled against this clear manifestation of the Lord's will, he would have withdrawn his light from me, and my portion would have been among the wicked, cast out forever from the favorable presence of my judge. I should also forever have been obliged to acknowledge his mercy and justice, and acquit the Lord, my redeemer, who had done so much for me; for with long-suffering and much abused mercy he had waited patiently for my return, and would have gathered me before that time, as I well knew, as a hen gathereth her chickens under her wings, but I would not." [2]

His second diversion, and probably practiced after he had given up dancing, was hunting. While not considered in itself reprehensible, when the sport led to wantonness,

[1] Journal of Elias Hicks, p. 10.

[2] Journal, p. 11.

and the taking of life of bird or beast simply for amusement, it was vigorously condemned. He says that he was
finally "led to consider conduct like this to be a great breach
of trust, and an infringement of the divine prerogative."
"It therefore became a settled principle with me not to take
the life of any creature, unless it was really useful and
necessary when dead, or very noxious and hurtful when
living." [3]

When the settled conviction came to him touching the
dance and the sportsman's practice, he was probably not out
of his teens. This conviction resulted in victory over the
propensity, probably before he reached his majority. The
whole experience was an early illustration of the strength
of will and purpose which was characteristic of this remarkable man throughout his entire life.

Marriage is always a turning-point in a man's life. In
the case of Elias Hicks, it was so in a marked degree.
Having become adept in his trade, at the age of twenty-
two, he was married to Jemima Seaman. This important
event cannot be better stated than in the simple, quaint language of the bridegroom himself. He says:

"My affection being drawn toward her in that relation,
I communicated my views to her, and received from her a
corresponding expression; and having the full unity and
concurrence of our parents and friends, we, after some time,
accomplished our marriage at a solemn meeting of Friends,
at Westbury, on the 2d of First month, 1771. On this
important occasion we felt the clear and consoling evidence
of divine truth, and it remained with us as a seal upon our
spirits, strengthening us mutually to bear, with becoming
fortitude, the vicissitudes and trials which fell to our lot,
and of which we had a large share while passing through
this probationary state." [4]

---

[3] Journal, p. 13.

[4] Journal, p. 13.

The records of Westbury Monthly Meeting contain the official evidence of this marriage, which was evidently conducted strictly in accordance with discipline. From the minutes of that meeting we extract the following:

"At a monthly meting held in the meeting house, ye 29th day of ye Eleventh month, 1770.

"Elias Hicks son of John Hicks, of Rockaway, and Jemima Seaman, daughter of Jonathan Seaman, of Jericho, presented themselves and declared their intentions of marriage with each, and this meeting appoints John Mott and Micajah Mott to make enquiry into Elias Hicks, his clearness in relation of marriage with other women, and to make report at the next monthly meeting.

"At a monthly meeting in the meeting house at Westbury ye 26th day of ye Twelfth month, 1770, Elias Hicks and Jemima Seaman appeared the second time, and Elias Hicks signified they continued their intentions of marriage and desired an answer to their former proposals of marriage, and the Friends who were appointed to make enquiry into Elias' clearness reported that they had made enquiry, and find nothing but that he is clear of marriage engagements to other women, and they having consent of parents and nothing appearing to obstruct their proceedings in marriage, this meeting leaves them to solemnize their marriage according to the good order used amongst Friends, and appoints Robert Seaman and John Mott to attend their said marriage, and to make report to the next monthly meeting it was consummated.

"On ye 30th day of ye First month, 1771, Robert Seaman reported that they had attended the marriage of Elias Hicks and Jemima Seaman, and was with them both at Jericho and at Rockaway, and John Mott also reported that he accompanied them at Rockaway and that the marriage was consummated orderly."

In more ways than one the marriage of Elias was the important event of his life. Jemima Seaman was an only child, and naturally her parents desired that she should be near them. A few months after their marriage Elias and Jemima were urged to take up their residence at the Seaman homestead, Elias to manage the farm of his father-in-law. The result was that the farm in Jericho became the home of Elias Hicks the remainder of his life. Here he lived and labored for nearly sixty years.

The Seamans were concerned Friends, and the farm was near the Friends' meeting house in Jericho. From this dates his constant attendance at the meetings for worship and discipline of the Society. Besides the family influence, some of his neighbors, strong men and women, and deeply attached to the principles and testimonies of Friends, made for the young people an ideal and inspiring environment. The Friends at Jericho could not have been unmindful of the native ability and taking qualities of this young man, whose fortunes were to be linked with their own, and whose future labors were to be so singularly devoted to their religious Society.

Jemima, the wife of Elias Hicks, was the daughter of Jonathan and Elizabeth Seaman. The father of Jemima was the fifth generation from Captain John Seaman, who came to Long Island from the Connecticut mainland about 1660. For his time, he seems to have been a man of affairs, and is recorded as one of the patentees of the town of Hempstead, on the Sound side of the island. There was a John Seaman who came to Massachusetts in the Winthrop fleet of ten vessels and 900 immigrants in 1630. That form of biography which shades into tradition is not agreed as to whether Captain John, of Hempstead, was the Puritan John or his son.

Running the family history back to England, we find Lazarus Seaman, known as a Puritan divine, a native of Leicester. He died in 1667. He is described as a learned theologian, versed in the art of controversy, and stout in defense of his position in religious matters.

The history of heraldry, and the story of the efforts

to capture the holy sepulcher, tell us that John de Seaman was one of the first crusaders. To this line the Seaman lineage in America is believed to be attached.

At some time, whether in his early manhood is not known, Elias Hicks took up surveying. How steadily or extensively he followed that business it is impossible to say. It is not hard, however, to find samples of his surveying and plotting along the papers of Long Island conveyancers.[5] His compass, and the home-made pine case in which he kept the instrument and the tripod, are in existence.[6] The compass is a simple affair, without a telescope, of course. It folds into a flat shape, the box not being more than two inches thick, over all.

---

[5] See cut facing page 145.

[6] They are in possession of the great-grandson of Elias Hicks, William Seaman, of Glen Cove, L. I.

CHAPTER III.

First Appearance in the Ministry.

THERE are many evidences in the Journal that Elias Hicks appreciated the moral and spiritual advantages of his environment after he took up his residence at Jericho. He confesses, however, that as he had entered quite extensively into business, he was much diverted from spiritual things for a number of years after his marriage. During this period he says:

"I was again brought, by the operative influence of divine grace, under deep concern of mind; and was led, through adorable mercy, to see that although I had ceased from many sins and vanities of my youth, yet there were many remaining that I was still guilty of, which were not yet atoned for, and for which I now felt the judgments of God to rest upon me. This caused me to cry earnestly to the Most High for pardon and redemption, and he graciously condescended to hear my cry, and to open a way before me, wherein I must walk, in order to experience reconciliation with him; and as I abode in watchfulness and deep humiliation before him, light broke forth out of obscurity, and my darkness became as the noonday. I had many deep openings in the visions of light, greatly strengthening and establishing to my exercised mind. My spirit was brought under a close and weighty labour in meetings for discipline, and my understanding much enlarged therein; and I felt a concern to speak to some of the subjects engaging the meeting's attention, which often brought unspeakable comfort to my mind. About this time I began to have openings leading to the ministry, which brought me under close exercise and deep travail of spirit; for although I had for some time spoken on subjects of business in monthly and preparative meetings, yet the prospect of opening my mouth in public meetings was a close trial; but I endeavored to keep my mind quiet and resigned to the heavenly call, if it should be made clear to me to be my duty. Nevertheless, as I was, soon after, sitting in a meeting, in much weightiness of spirit, a secret, though clear, intimation accompanied me to speak a few words, which were then given to me to utter, yet fear so prevailed that I did not yield to the intimation. For this omission I felt close rebuke, and judgment seemed, for some time, to cover my mind; but as I humbled myself under the Lord's mighty hand, he again lifted up the light of his countenance upon me, and enabled me to renew covenant with him, that if he would pass by this offense, I would, in the future, be faithful, if he should again require such a service of me. And it was not long before I felt an impressive concern to utter a few words, which I yielded to in great fear and dread; but oh, the joy and sweet consolation that my soul experienced, as a reward for this act of faithfulness; and as I continued persevering in duty and watchfulness, I witnessed an increase in divine knowledge, and an enlargement of my gift. I was also deeply engaged for the right administration of discipline and order in the church, and that all might be kept sweet and clean, consitent with the nature and purity of the holy profession we were making; so that all stumbling-blocks might be removed out of the way of honest inquirers, and that truth's testimony might be exalted, and the Lord's name magnified, 'who is over all, God blessed forever.' "[1]

Still it appears that his concern for the maintenance of the discipline was more than a slavish allegiance to the letter of the law. More than once he spoke a warning word as to the danger of allowing the administration of the written rule to lead to mere formalism. Once begun, his development in public service was rapid, and his recognition by Friends cordial and appreciative to a marked degree.

Just how long Elias Hicks spoke in the meetings for worship, before his "acknowledgment," is not known. The records of Westbury Monthly Meeting, however, give de-

---

[1] Journal, p. 15.

tailed information as to this event. From them we make the following extract:

"At a monthly meeting held at Westbury ye 29th of Fourth month, 1778, William Seaman and William Valentine report that they have made inquiry concerning Elias Hicks, and find nothing to hinder his being recommended to the meeting of Ministers and Elders, whom this meeting recommends to that meeting as a minister, and directs the clerk to forward a copy of this minute to said meeting."

The acknowledgment of the ministry of Elias Hicks took place a little over seven years after his marriage. From various references in the Journal the inference is warranted that he did not begin to speak in the meeting for worship until a considerable time after this event. It is, therefore, probable that his service in this line had not been going on, at the most, more than three or four years when his acknowledgment took place. He had only been a recorded minister something over a year when his first considerable visit was undertaken.

Unfortunately, the preserved personal correspondence of Elias Hicks does not cover this period in his life, so that we are confined to what he chose to put in his Journal, as the only self-interpretation of this interesting period.

It appears that the New York Yearly Meeting was held at the regularly appointed times all through the period of the Revolutionary War. Previous to 1777 the meeting met annually at Flushing, but in that year the sessions were removed to Westbury. In 1793 it was concluded to hold future meetings in New York.

During the war the British controlled Long Island, and for some time the meeting house in Flushing was occupied as a barracks by the king's troops, which probably accounts for moving the yearly meeting further out on the island to Westbury.

In attending the yearly meeting, and in performing

religious visits to the particular meetings, passing the lines of both armies was a frequent necessity. This privilege was freely granted Friends. Touching this matter, Elias makes this reference:

"This was a favor which the parties would not grant to their best friends, who were of a warlike disposition; which shows what great advantages would redound to mankind were they all of this pacific spirit. I passed myself through the lines of both armies six times during the war without molestation, both parties generally receiving me with openness and civility; and although I had to pass over a tract of country, between the two armies, sometimes more than thirty miles in extent, and which was much frequented by robbers, a set, in general, of cruel, unprincipled banditti, issuing out from both parties, yet, excepting once, I met with no interruption even from them. But although Friends in general experienced many favors and deliverances, yet those scenes of war and confusion occasioned many trials and provings in various ways to the faithful." [2]

---

[2] Journal. p. 15.

CHAPTER IV.

Early Labors in the Ministry.

PROBABLY the first official public service to which Elias Hicks was ever assigned by the Society related to a matter growing out of the Revolutionary War. Under the new meeting-house in New York was a large room, usually rented for commercial purposes. During the British occupation this room was appropriated as a storehouse for military goods. The rent was finally tendered by the military commissioner to some representative Friends, and by them accepted. This caused great concern to many members of the meeting, who felt that the Society of Friends could not consistently be the recipient of money from such a source. The matter came before the Yearly Meeting in 1779. The peace party felt that the rent money was blood money, and should be returned, but a vigorous minority sustained the recipients of this warlike revenue. It was finally decided to refer the matter to the Yearly Meeting of Pennsylvania for determination. A committee to carry the matter to Philadelphia was appointed, of which Elias Hicks, then a young man of thirty-one, was a member.

He made this service the occasion for some religious visits, which he, in company with his friend, John Willis, proceeded to make *en route*. The two Friends left home the Ninth month 9, 1779, but took a roundabout route in order to visit the meetings involved in the concern of Elias. Instead of crossing over into New Jersey and going directly to Philadelphia, they went up the Hudson valley to a point above Newburgh, visiting meetings on both sides of the river. Their most northern point was the meeting at Marlborough, in Ulster County, New York. They then turned to the southwest, and visited the meetings at Hardwick [1] and Kingwood, arriving at Philadelphia, Ninth month 25th. Elias attended all the sittings of the yearly meeting until Fourth-day, when he was taken ill, and was not able to be in attendance after that time. He was not present when the matter which called the committee to Philadelphia was considered. The decision, however, was that the money received by the New York meeting for rent paid by the British army should be returned. This was done by direction of New York Yearly Meeting in 1780. It may be interesting to note that in 1779 the Yearly Meeting of Pennsylvania began with the Meeting of Ministers and Elders, Seventh-day, the 25th of Ninth month, and continued until Second-day, the 4th of Tenth month, having practically. been in session a week and two days.[2]

Following the Yearly Meeting in Philadelphia, the meeting at Byberry was visited, as were those at Wrightstown, Plumstead and Buckingham, in Bucks County, Pa. On the return trip be was again at Hardwick, after which he passed to the eastern shore of the Hudson, and was at Nine Partners, Oswego and Oblong. Turning southward, the meetings at Peach Pond, Amawalk and Purchase were visited. From the latter point he journeyed homeward.

This first religious journey of Elias Hicks lasted nine weeks, and in making it he traveled 860 miles. Forty years later, many of the places visited at this time became centers of the troublesome controversy which divided the Society in 1827 and 1828.

Four years after the concern and service which took

---

[1] Hardwick was in Sussex County, New Jersey. It was the home meeting of Benjamin Lundy, the abolitionist.

[2] From 1755 to 1798, Philadelphia Yearly Meeting was held in Ninth month.

Elias Hicks to Philadelphia in 1779, he undertook his second recorded religious visit. It was a comparatively short one, and took him to the Nine Partners neighborhood. He was absent from home on this trip eleven days, and traveled 170 miles.

In 1784 Elias had a concern to visit neighborhoods in Long Island not Friendly in their character. He made one trip, and not feeling free of the obligations resting upon him, he made a second tour. During the two visits he rode about 200 miles.

He seems to have had a period of quiet home service for about six years, or until 1790, when two somewhat extended concerns were followed. The first took him to the meetings in the western part of Long Island, to New York City and Staten Island. This trip caused him to travel 150 miles. The next visiting tour covered a wide extent of territory, and took him to eastern New York and Vermont. On this trip he was gone from home about four weeks, and traveled 591 miles.

The year 1791 was more than usually active. Besides another visit to those not Friends on Long Island, he made a general visit to Friends in New York Yearly Meeting. This visit took him to New Jersey, Connecticut, Massachusetts and up the Hudson valley as far as Easton and Saratoga. The Long Island visit consumed two weeks' time, and involved traveling 115 miles. On the general visit he was absent from home four months and eleven days, and traveled 1500 miles.

In 1792 a committee, of which Elias was a member, was appointed by the Yearly Meeting of Ministers and Elders to visit subordinate meetings of that branch of the Society. In company with these Friends every meeting of Ministers and Elders was visited, and a number of meetings for worship were attended. On this trip he was at

Claremont, in Massachusetts, and desired to have an appointed meeting. It seemed that the person, not a Friend, who was to arrange for this meeting did not advertise it, for fear it would turn out a silent meeting, and he would be laughed to scorn. The attendance was very small, but otherwise satisfactory, so that the fearful person was very penitent, and desired that another meeting might be held. Elias says: "But we let him know that we were not at our own disposal; and, as no way appeared open in our minds for such an appointment at present, we could not comply with his desire."

An appointed meeting was also held near Dartmouth College, but the students were hilarious, and the occasion very much disturbed. Still, the visitor hoped "the season was profitable to some present."

In the following year, 1793, he had a concern to visit Friends in New England, during which he attended meetings in Rhode Island, Connecticut, Massachusetts, Maine and the Massachusetts islands. On this trip he traveled by land or on water 2283 miles, and was absent about five months. It may be interesting to note that the traveling companion of Elias Hicks on the New England visit was James Mott, of Mamaroneck, N. Y., the maternal grand-father of James Mott, the husband of Lucretia.

The New England Yearly Meeting was attended at Newport. The meeting was pronounced a "dull time" by the visitor. This was occasioned in part, he thought, because a very small number took upon them the whole man-agement of the business, and thereby shutting up the way to others, and preventing the free circulation and spreading of the concern, in a proper manner, on the minds of Friends;

---

[3]Adam Mott, the father of Lucretia's husband, married Anne, daughter of James Mott.

which I have very often found to be a very hurtful tendency."

It seems that in those days the Meeting of Ministers and Elders exercised the functions of a visiting committee. Accordingly, the Yearly Meeting of Ministers and Elders in 1795 appointed a committee to visit the quarterly and preparative meetings within the bounds of the Yearly Meeting. As a member of this committee, Elias performed his share of this round of service. On this visit a large number of families were visited.

The visits were made seasons of counsel and advice, especially in the "select meetings." In these, he says, "My mind was led to communicate some things in a plain way, with a view of stirring them up to more diligence and circumspection in their families, the better ordering and disciplining of their children and household, and keeping things sweet and clean, agreeably to the simplicity of our holy profession; and I had peace in my labor." [4]

Possibly his most extended visit up to that time was made in 1798. The trip was really begun Twelfth month 12, 1797. It included meetings in New Jersey, Pennsylvania, Delaware, Maryland and Virginia. On this trip he was from home five and one-half months, traveled 1600 miles, and attended 143 meetings, nearly an average of one meeting a day.

It was on this journey that he seriously began his public opposition to the institution of slavery. On the 12th of Third month, at a meeting at Elk Ridge, Md., he says:

"Truth rose into dominion, and some present who were slave-holders were made sensible of their condition, and were much affected. I felt a hope to arise that the opportunity would prove profitable to some, and I left them with peace of mind. Since then I have been informed that a woman present at that session, who possessed a number of slaves, was so fully convinced, as to set them free, and not long afterwards joined in membership with Friends; which is indeed cause of gratitude and thankfulness of heart, to the great and blessed Author of every mercy vouchsafed to the children of men." [5]

His personal correspondence on this trip yields some interesting description of experiences, from which we take the following extract, from a letter written to his wife from "Near Easton, Talbot County, Maryland, Second month 12, 1798":

"Mary Berry, an ancient ministering Friend, that Job Scott makes mention of, was with us at the meeting. On Seventh-day we attended a meeting with the black people at Easton, which we had appointed some days before. There was a pretty large number attended, and the opportunity favored. Mary Berry observed she thought it was the most so, of any that had ever been with them. They were generally very solid, and many of them very tender. The white people complained much of some of them for their bad conduct, but according to my feeling, many of them appeared much higher in the kingdom than a great many of the whites.

"Some days past we were with the people called Nicolites. They dress very plain, many of them mostly in white. The women wore white bonnets as large as thine, and in form like thy old-fashioned bonnet, straight and smooth on the top. In some of their meetings three or four of the foremost seats would be filled with those who mostly had on these white bonnets. They have no backs to their seats, nor no rising seats in their meeting-houses. All sat on a level. They appear like a pretty honest, simple people. Profess our principles, and most of them, by their request, have of late been joined to Friends, and I think many of them are likely to become worthy members of Society, if the example of the backsliders among us do not stumble or turn them out of the right way. There was about 100 received by Friends here at their last monthly meeting, and are like for the first time to attend here next Fifth-day, which made it the more pressing on my mind to tarry over that day."

[5] Journal, p. 67.

CHAPTER V.

Later Ministerial Labors.

IN THE fall of 1799 a concern to visit meetings in Connecticut was followed. The trip also took in most of the meetings on the east bank of the Hudson as far north as Dutchess County. He was absent six weeks, and attended thirty meetings.

Fourth month 11, 1801, Elias and his traveling companion, Edmund Willis, started on a visit to "Friends in some parts of Jersey, Pennsylvania, and some places adjacent thereto." A number of meetings in New Jersey were visited on the way, the travelers arriving in Philadelphia in time for the Yearly Meeting of Ministers and Elders. All of the sessions of the yearly meeting were also attended. It does not appear that Elias Hicks had attended this yearly meeting since 1779. Practically all of the meetings in New Jersey and Pennsylvania were visited on this trip. It lasted three months and eighteen days, during which time the visitors traveled 1630 miles.

The personal correspondence of Elias Hicks yields one interesting letter written on this trip. It was written to his wife, and was dated "Exeter, 4th of Seventh month, 1801." We quote as follows:

"We did not get to Lampeter so soon as I expected. as mentioned in my last, for when we left Yorktown last Fourth-day evening, being late before we set out, detained in part by a shower of rain. It was night by the time we got over the river. We landed in a little town called Columbia, where dwelt a few friends. Although being anxious to get forward. I had previous to coming there intended to pass them without a meeting, but found when there I could

38

not safely do it. Therefore we appointed a meeting there the next day, after which we rode to Lampeter, to William Brinton's, of whom, when I went westward, I got a fresh horse, and I left mine in his care. I have now my own again, but she has a very bad sore on her withers, something like is called a 'thistlelon,' but is better than she has been. It is now just six weeks and four days since we went from this place, which is about 48 miles from Philadelphia, since which time we have rode 813 miles and attended 35 meetings. Much of the way in this tour has been rugged, mountainous and rocky, and had it not been for the best attendant companion, peace of mind flowing from a compliance with and performance of manifested duty, the journey would have been tedious and irksome. But we passed pretty cheerfully on, viewing with an attentive eye the wonderful works of that boundless wisdom and power (by which the worlds were framed) and which are only circumscribed within the limits of their own innate excellency. Here we beheld all nature almost with its varied and almost endless diversifications.

"Tremendous precipices, rocks and mountains, creeks and rivers, intersecting each other, all clothed in their natural productions; the tall pines and sturdy oaks towering their exalted heads above the clouds, interspersed with beautiful lawns and glades; together with the almost innumerable vegetable inhabitants, all blooming forth the beauties of the spring; the fields arable, clothed in rich pastures of varied kinds, wafted over the highways their balmy sweets, and the fallow grounds overspread with rich grain, mostly in golden wheat, to a profusion beyond anything of the kind my eyes ever before beheld, insomuch that the sensible traveler, look which way he would, could scarcely help feeling his mind continually inflamed and inspired with humble gratitude and reverent thankfulness to the great and bountiful author of all those multiplied blessings."

This letter constitutes one of the few instances where Elias Hicks referred to experiences on the road, not directly connected with his ministerial duty. The reference to Columbia, and his original intention to pass by without a meeting, with its statement he "could not safely do it," is characteristic. Manifestly, he uses the word "safely" in a spiritual sense. The call to minister there was too certain to be put aside for mere personal inclination and comfort.

The reference to his horse contains more than a passing interest. Probably many other cases occurred during his visits when "borrowing" a horse was necessary, while his own was recuperating. It was a slow way to travel, from our standpoint, yet it had its advantages. New acquaintances, if not friendships, were made as the travelers journeyed and were entertained on the road.

On the 20th of Ninth month, 1803, Elias Hicks, with Daniel Titus as a traveling companion, started on a visit to Friends in Upper Canada, and those resident in the part of the New York Yearly Meeting located in the Hudson and Mohawk valleys. When the travelers had been from home a little less than a month, Elias wrote to his wife, from Kingston, a letter of more than ordinary interest, because of its descriptive quality. It describes some of the difficulties, not to say dangers, of the traveling Friend before the days of railroads. We quote the bulk of the letter, which was dated Tenth month, 16, 1803:

"We arrived here the 3d instant at the house of Joseph Ferris about 3 o'clock at night, having rode the preceding day from Samuel Brown's at Black River, where I dated my last. We traveled by land and water in this day's journey about forty-five miles. Very bad traveling over logs and mudholes, crossing two ferries on our way, each four or five miles wide, with an island between called Long Island. About six miles across we were in the middle thereof, the darkest time in the night, when we were under the necessity of getting off our horses several times to feel for the horses' tracks in order to know whether we were in the path or not, as we were not able to see the path, nor one another at times, if more than five or six feet apart. Some of our company began to fear we should be under the necessity of lying in the woods all night. However, we were favored to get well through, and crossed the last ferry about midnight and after. Landed safely on Kingston shore about 2 o'clock, all well. Since which we have attended ten meetings, three of them preparative meetings, the rest mostly among other people. We just now, this evening, returned from the last held at the house of John Everit, about four miles west of Kingston. We held one yesterday in the town of Kingston in their Court House. It was the first Friends' meeting ever held in that place. The principal inhabitants generally attended, and we have thankfully to acknowledge that the shepherd of Israel in whom was our trust, made bare his arm for our help, setting home the testimony he gave us to the states of the people, thereby manifesting that he had not 'left himself without a witness in their hearts, as all appeared to yield their assent to the truths delivered, which has generally been the case, in every place where our lots have been cast.

"We expect to-morrow to return on our way to Adolphustown, taking some meetings in our way thither, among those not of our Society, but so as to be there ready to attend Friends' monthly that is held next Fifth-day, after which we have some prospect of being at liberty to return on our way back, into our own State.

"Having thus given thee a short account of our journey, I may salute thee in the fresh feelings of endeared affection, and strength of gospel love, in which fervent desires are felt for thy preservation, and that of our dear children, and that you may all so act and so walk, as to be a comfort and strength to each other, and feel an evidence in yourselves that the Lord is your friend; for you are my friend (said the blessed redeemer) if you do whatever I command you."

For the three following years there is no record of special activity, but in 1806 a somewhat extended visit was made to Friends in the State of New York. He was absent from home nearly two months, traveled over 1000 miles, attended three quarterly, seventeen monthly, sixteen preparative, and forty meetings for worship.

The years following, including 1812, were spent either at home or in short, semi-occasional visits, mostly within the bounds of his own yearly meeting. During this period a visit to Canada Half-Yearly Meeting was made.

The first half of 1813 he was busy in his business and . domestic concerns, really preparing for a religious journey, which he began on the 8th of Fifth month. He passed through New Jersey on the way, attending meetings in that State, either regular or by appointment, arriving in Philadelphia in about two weeks. Several meetings in the vicinity of that city were attended, whence he passed into Delaware and Maryland. His steps were retraced through New Jersey, when he was homeward bound.

From 1813 to 1816 we find the gospel labors of Elias Hicks almost entirely confined to his own yearly meeting. This round of service did not take him farther from home than Dutchess County. During this period we find him repeatedly confessing indisposition and bodily ailment, which may have accounted for the fewness and moderateness of his religious visits.

In First month, 1816, we find him under a concern to visit Friends in New England. He had as his traveling companion on this journey his friend and kinsman, Isaac Hicks, of Westbury. During this trip practically all of the meetings in New England were visited. It kept him from home about three months, and caused him to travel upward of 1000 miles. He attended fifty-nine particular, three monthly and two quarterly meetings.

During the balance of 1816 and part of the year 1817, service was principally confined to the limits of Westbury Quarterly Meeting. But it was in no sense, a period of idleness. Many visits were made to meetings. In Eighth month of the latter year, in company with his son-in-law, Valentine Hicks, a visit was made to some of the meetings attached to Philadelphia and Baltimore Yearly Meetings. Many meetings in New Jersey and Pennsylvania received a visit at this time. He went as far south as Loudon County, Va., taking meetings *en route,* both going and coming. He must have traveled not less than 1000 miles on this trip.

Visits near at home, and one to some parts of New York Yearly Meeting, occupied all his time during the year 1818.

In 1819 a general visit to Friends in his own yearly meeting engaged his attention. He went to the Canadian border. This trip was a season of extended service and deep exercise. On this journey he traveled 1084 miles, was absent from home fourteen weeks, and attended seventy-three meetings for worship, three quarterly meetings and four monthly meetings.

The years from 1819 to 1823, inclusive, were particularly active. Elias Hicks was seventy-one in the former year. The real stormy period of his life was approaching in the shape of the unfortunate misunderstanding and bitterness which divided the Society. It scarcely demands more than passing mention here, as later on we shall give deserved prominence to the "separation" period.

He started on the Ohio trip Eighth month 17, 1819, taking northern and central Pennsylvania on his route. He arrived in Mt. Pleasant in time for Ohio Yearly Meeting, which seems to have been a most satisfactory occasion, with no signs of the storm that broke over the same meeting a few years later. Elias himself says: "It was thought, I believe, by Friends, to have been the most favored yearly meeting they had had since its institution, and was worthy of grateful remembrance." [1] During this visit many appointed meetings were held, besides regular meetings for worship. On the homeward journey, Friends in the Shenandoah Valley, in Virginia, and in parts of Maryland were visited.

---

[1] Journal, p. 377.

On this trip he journeyed 1200 miles, was from home three months, and attended eighty-seven meetings.

In 1820 a visit was made to Farmington and Duanesburg Quarterly Meetings, and in the summer of 1822 he visited Friends in some parts of Philadelphia Yearly Meeting. On this trip the Baltimore Yearly Meeting was also visited, as were some of the particular meetings in Maryland. He did not reach Philadelphia on the return journey until the early part of Twelfth month. While his Journal is singularly silent about the matter, it must have been on this visit that he encountered his first public opposition as a minister. But, with few exceptions, the Journal ignores the whole unpleasantness.

In 1824 he again attended Baltimore Yearly Meeting. The only comment on this trip is the following: "I think it was, in its several sittings, one of the most satisfactory yearly meetings I have ever attended, and the business was conducted in much harmony and brotherly love." [2]

On the homeward trip he stopped in Philadelphia. Here he suffered a severe illness. Of this detention at that time he says: "I lodged at the house of my kind friend, Samuel R. Fisher, who, with his worthy children, extended to me the most affectionate care and attention; and I had also the kind sympathy of a large portion of Friends in that city." [3] The exception contained in this sentence is the only intimation that all was not unity and harmony among Friends in the "City of Brotherly Love."

His visits in 1825 were confined to the meetings on Long Island and those in central New York.

In the latter part of the following year he secured a

---

[2] Journal, p. 396.

[3] Journal, p. 396.

minute to visit meetings composing Concord and Southern Quarterly Meetings, within the bounds of Philadelphia Yearly Meeting. In passing through Philadelphia he attended Green Street and Mulberry Street Meetings. This was within a few months of the division of 1827 in Philadelphia Yearly Meeting, but the latter is not mentioned in the Journal.

CHAPTER VI.

Religious Journeys in 1828.

On the 20th of Third month, 1828, Elias Hicks laid before Jericho Monthly Meeting a concern he had to make "a religious visit in the love of the gospel, to Friends and others in some parts of our own yearly meeting, and in the compass of the Yearly Meetings of Philadelphia, Baltimore, Ohio, Indiana, and a few meetings in Virginia." A minute embodying this concern was granted him, the same receiving the indorsement of Westbury Quarterly Meeting, Fourth month 24th. Between this period and the middle of Sixth month he made a visit to Dutchess County, where the experience with Ann Jones and her husband took place, which will be dealt with in a separate chapter. He also attended New York Yearly Meeting, when he saw and was a part of the "separation" trouble which culminated at that time. The Journal, however, makes no reference either to the Dutchess County matter or to the division in the yearly meeting. These silences in the Journal are hard to understand. Undoubtedly, the troubles of the period were not pleasant matters of record, yet one wishes that a fuller and more detailed statement regarding the whole matter might be had from Elias Hicks than is contained in the meager references in his personal correspondence, or his published Journal.

On the 14th of Sixth month he started on the western and southern journey, with his friend, Jesse Merritt, as his traveling companion. Elias was then a few months past eighty.

The two Friends halted at points in New Jersey and Pennsylvania, holding meetings as the way opened. Service continued in Pennsylvania, considerably in the western part, passing from Pittsburg into Ohio.

At Westland Monthly Meeting, in Pennsylvania, his first acknowledgment of opposition is observed. He says: "A Friend from abroad attended this meeting, and after I sat down he rose and made opposition, which greatly disturbed the meeting."[1]

When he arrived at Brownsville, his fame had preceded him. He makes this reference to the experience there:

"Here we put up again with our kind friends Jesse and Edith Townsend, where we had the company of many Friends, and many of the inhabitants of the town not members of our Society, also came in to see us; as the unfounded reports of those who style themselves Orthodox, having been generally spread over the country, it created such a great excitement in the minds of the people at large, that multitudes flocked to the meetings where we were, to hear for themselves; and many came to see us, and acknowledged their satisfaction.

"At this place we again fell in with the Friend from abroad, who attended the meeting with us; he rose in the early part of the meeting, and continued his communication so long that a number left the meeting, by which it became very much unsettled: however, when he sat down I felt an opening to stand up; and the people returned and crowded into the house, and those that could not get in stood about the doors and windows, and a precious solemnity soon spread over the meeting, which has been the case in every meeting, where our opposers did not make disturbance by their disorderly conduct. The meeting closed in a quiet and orderly manner, and I was very thankful for the favour."[2]

Following his experience at Brownsville, Elias returned to Westland, attending the meeting of ministers and elders, and the meeting for worship. The person before

---

[1] Thomas Shillitoe.

[2] Journal, p. 404.

mentioned, who may be called the "disturbing Friend," was
again in evidence, this time reinforced by a "companion."
At the instigation of Friends, the elders and overseers had
"an opportunity" with the disturbers, but with small success.   The same trouble was repeated on First-day.   On
this occasion the opposition was vigorous and virulent.   In
the midst of the second opportunity of the opposing Friend
the audience melted away, leaving him literally without
hearers.

From Westland the journey was continued to Pittsburg, where an appointed meeting was held.   Salem, Ohio,
was the next point visited, where the quarterly meeting was
attended.   On First-day a large company, estimated at
two thousand, gathered.   The occasion was in every way
satisfactory.   Visits to different meetings continued.   There
was manifest opposition at New Garden, Springfield,
Gosnen and Marlborough.   At Smithfield the venerable
preacher was quite indisposed.   The meeting-house was
closed against him, by "those called Orthodox," as Elias
defined them.

One of the objective points on this trip was Mt. Pleasant, Ohio, where the yearly meeting of 1828 was held.
He arrived in time to attend the mid-week meeting at that
place, a week preceding the yearly meeting.   A large
attendance was reported, many being present who were not
members of the Society.   The signs of trouble had preceded
the distinguished visitor, the "world's people" having a
phenomenal curiosity regarding a possible war among the
peaceable Quakers.   There was pronounced antagonism
manifested in this mid-week meeting, described as "a long,
tedious communication from a minister among those called
Orthodox, who, after I sat down, publicly opposed and
endeavored to lay waste what I had said." [3]

---

[3] Journal, p. 411.

During the following days meetings were attended at Short Creek, Harrisville, West Grove, Concord, St. Clairsville, Plainfield, Wrightstown and Stillwater. There was no recorded disturbance until he returned to Mt. Pleasant the 6th of Ninth month, the date of the gathering of the Yearly Meeting of Ministers and Elders. When the meeting-house was reached the gate to the yard was guarded, "by a number of men of the opposing party," who refused entrance to those who were in sympathy with Elias Hicks. They proceeded to hold their meeting in the open air. Subsequent meetings were held in a school-house and in a private house, the home of Israel French.

First-day, Ninth month 7th, Mt. Pleasant Meeting was attended in the forenoon, and Short Creek Meeting in the afternoon. The meeting at Mt. Pleasant was what might be called stormy. Elisha Bates and Ann Braithwaite spoke in opposition, after Elias Hicks had spoken. In a letter dated Ninth month 10th, written to his son-in-law, Valentine Hicks, Elias says that these Friends "detained the meeting two hours or more, opposing and railing against what I had said, until the people were wearied and much disgusted." No trouble was experienced at Short Creek, although experiences similar to those of the morning occurred at Mt. Pleasant in the afternoon. Amos Peaslee, of Woodbury, N. J., was the center of opposition at that time. He was opposed while on his feet addressing the multitude.

In connection with this yearly meeting a number of Friends were arrested on charges of trespass and inducing a riot, and taken to court. All were members of Ohio Yearly Meeting, except Halliday Jackson,[4] of Darby, Pa.

---

[4] Halliday Jackson was father of John Jackson, the well-known educator, principal of Sharon Hill School. Halliday was with the Seneca Indians in New York State for two years, as a teacher under the care of Philadelphia Yearly Meeting.   7

For some reason Elias escaped arrest, although in the letter referred to he said: "I have been expecting for several days past to have a writ of trespass served against me by the sheriff, for going on their meeting-house grounds, by which I may be taken twenty miles or more to appear before the judge, as a number of Friends already have been, although my mind is quiet regarding the event."

While at Mt. Pleasant the small monthly meeting of Orthodox Friends at his home sent a letter "officially" commanding Elias to cease his religious visits. In regard to this matter, and the general situation in Ohio, Elias wrote to Valentine Hicks: "The Orthodox in this yearly meeting are, if possible, tenfold more violent than in any other part of the Society. Gideon Seaman, and his associates in the little upstart Monthly Meeting of Westbury and Jericho,[5] have sent a very peremptory order for me to return immediately home, and not proceed any further on my religious visit, by which they trample the authority of our quarterly and monthly meeting under foot."

Following the Ohio Yearly Meeting, Flushing,[6] in that State, was visited, and the First-day meeting attended. Elias was met before he reached the meeting-house by Orthodox Friends, who insisted that he should not interrupt the meeting. He entered the house, but before the meeting was fairly settled, Charles Osborn, an Orthodox Friend, appeared in prayer, and continued for an hour; and then preached for another hour. Elias thus refers to this occurrence:

"However, when he sat down, although the meeting was much wearied with his long and tedious communica-

[5] The Monthly Meeting of Westbury and Jericho was made up of a small number of Orthodox Friends, representing only a small minority of the meeting of which Elias Hicks was a member.

[6] Flushing is about 18 miles from Mt. Pleasant. A Wilburite meeting is the only Friendly gathering now in the place.

tions, I felt the necessity of standing up and addressing the people, which brought a precious solemnity over the meeting; but as soon as I sat down, he rose again to contradict, and tried to lay waste my communication, by asserting that I had not the unity of my friends at home; which being untrue, I therefore informed the meeting that I had certificates with me to prove the incorrectness of his assertions, which I then produced, but he and his party would not stay to hear them, but in a disorderly manner arose and left the meeting; but the people generally stayed and heard them read, to their general satisfaction."[7]

Meetings were subsequently attended at different points in Ohio, generally without disturbance, until Springfield was reached the 22d of Ninth month. Here the Orthodox shut the meeting-house and guarded the doors. Elias held his meeting under some trees nearby. He says: "It was a precious season, wherein the Lord's power and love were exalted over all opposition."[8]

Preceding Indiana Yearly Meeting, he was twice at Wilmington, Ohio, and attended monthly meeting at Center, the first held since the "separation." The attendance was large, many more than the house would accommodate. Elias says: "The Lord, our never-failing helper, manifested his presence, solemnizing the assembly and opening the minds of the people to receive the word preached; breaking down all opposition, and humbling and contriting the assembly in a very general manner."[9]

Ninth month 27th, Indiana Yearly Meeting convened at Waynesville, Ohio. It should be noted that the "separation" in most of the meetings comprising this yearly meeting had been accomplished in 1827, so that the gather-

---

[7] Journal, p. 414.

[8] Journal, p. 416.

[9] Journal, p. 415.

ing in 1828 was in substantial unity with the Friends in sympathy with Elias Hicks. A letter written to Valentine and Abigail Hicks, dated Waynesville, Tenth month 3, 1828, contains some interesting information concerning the experience of the venerable preacher. He says:

"The Yearly Meeting here would have been very large, had there not been a failure of the information of the conclusion for holding it here, reaching divers of the Quarterly Meetings, by which they were prevented from attending. The meeting was very orderly conducted, and the business managed in much harmony and condescension. The public meetings have been very large, favoured seasons, and all the meetings we have attended in our passing along have been generally very large. Seldom any houses were found large enough to contain the people. Often hundreds were under the necessity of standing out doors. Many of the people without came a great way to be at our meeting. Some ten, some twenty, and some thirty miles, and I have been informed since I have been here that the people in a town 120 miles below Cincinnati have given it in charge to Friends of that place to inform them when we came there, as a steam boat plies between the two places. The excitement is so great among the people by the false rumors circulated by the Orthodox, that they spare no pains to get an opportunity to be with us, and those who have attended from distant parts, informing the people the satisfaction they have had in being with us, in which they have found that the reports spread among them were generally false, it has increased the excitement in others to see for themselves."

The yearly meeting over, Elias attended meetings *en route* to Richmond, Ind., and was at the mid-week meeting in that place, Tenth month 8th. Several other meetings were attended, the only disturbance reported being at Orange, where the Orthodox "hurt the meeting very considerably." On the 19th he was in Cincinnati, and attended the regular meeting in the morning, and a large appointed meeting in the court-house in the afternoon. Both were pronounced "highly favored seasons."

First-day, the 26th, he was at Fairfield, where the

Orthodox revived the story that he was traveling without a minute. While Elias was speaking, the Orthodox left the meeting in a body. He remarks: "But Friends and others kept their seats, and we had a very solemn close, and great brokenness and contrition were manifest among the people; and to do away with the false report spread by the Orthodox, I had my certificates read, which gave full satisfaction to the assembly." [10]

Elias then journeyed to Wheeling, his face being turned homeward. He held an appointed meeting in that city. It is suggestive that, notwithstanding the theological odium under which he was supposed to rest, the meeting was held in the Methodist church, which had been kindly offered for the purpose. This would seem to indicate that the Methodists had not yet taken any sides in the quarrel which had divided the Society of Friends.

After visiting Redstone Quarterly Meeting, in western Pennsylvania, he visited the meetings in the Shenandoah and Loudon valleys, in Virginia. He was at Alexandria and Washington, and on First-day, Eleventh month 16th, was at Sandy Spring, Md. The meetings about Baltimore and in Harford and Cecil counties were visited. He reached West Grove in Pennsylvania, Twelfth month 1st, and encountered some trouble, as he found that the meeting-house had been closed against him. A large crowd assembled, better councils prevailed, and the house was opened. The audience was beyond the capacity of the house, and the meeting in every way satisfactory.

Upon his arrival at West Grove, Twelfth month 1st, he sent a letter to his son-in-law and daughter, Royal and Martha Aldrich. In this letter he gives a brief account of his experiences in Maryland and Lancaster County. He says: "The aforesaid meetings were very large and highly

---

[10] Journal, p. 419.

favored, generally made up of every description of people, high and low, rich and poor, Romanists, and generally some of every profession of Protestants known in our country. Generally all went away fully satisfied as to those evil reports that have been spread over the country concerning me, and many announced the abhorrence they had of those false and slanderous reports."

It appears from this letter that the traveling companion of Elias, Jesse Merritt, was homesick, and hoped that some other Friend would come from Long Island to take his place for the rest of the trip. In case such a shift was made, Elias requested that whoever came "might bring with him my best winter tight-bodied coat, and two thicker neck-cloths, as those I have are rather thin. I got a new great-coat in Alexandria, and shall not need any other."

From a letter written to his wife from West Chester, Twelfth month 7th, we learn that John Hicks had arrived to take the place of Jesse Merritt, and he seized that oppor-tunity to send a letter home. As the two Friends had been away from home nearly six months, it is not strange that the companion on this journey desired to return. He could scarcely have been under the deep and absorbing religious concern which was felt by his elder brother in the truth. The nature of this obligation is revealed in the letter last noted. In this epistle to his wife, Elias says:

"Abigail's letter informs of the infirm state of V. and Caroline, which excites near-feeling and sympathy with them, and which would induce me to return home imme-diately if I was set at liberty from my religious obligations, but as that is not the case, I can only recommend them to the preserving care and compassionate regard of our Heavenly Father, whose mercy is over all his works and does not suffer a sparrow to fall without his notice. And as we become resigned to his heavenly disposals, he will cause all things to work together for good, to his truly devoted children. Therefore, let all trust in him, for in the Lord Jehovah is everlasting strength."

The meetings in Delaware, eastern Pennsylvania and New Jersey were pretty generally attended, and with no reported disturbance. First-day, the 21st of Twelfth month, Elias attended the meeting at Cherry Street in the morning and Green Street in the afternoon, and on the 28th he repeated that experience. On both occasions "hundreds more assembled than the houses could contain." [11] In the suburban meetings in Delaware and Bucks Counties, "the houses were generally too small to contain the people; many had to stand out-of-doors for want of room; nevertheless, the people behaved orderly and the Lord was felt to preside, solemnizing those crowded assemblies, in all of which my mind was opened, and ability afforded, to preach the gospel to the people in the demonstration of the spirit and with power, and many hearts were broken and contrited and went away rejoicing, under thankful sense of the unmerited favor." [12]

The great crowds which flocked to hear Elias Hicks after the "separation" were probably called together partly because of curiosity on their part, and to a considerable extent because of his continued popularity as a minister, in spite of the trouble which had come to the Society. That he was appreciative of what we would now call the advertising quality of those who antagonized him, and became his theological and personal enemies, is well attested. In summing up his conclusions regarding the long religious visit now under review, he said: "My opposing brethren had, by their public opposition and erroneous reports, created such excitement in the minds of the people generally of every profession, that it induced multitudes to assemble to hear for themselves, and they generally went away satis-

[11] Journal, p. 423.

[12] Journal, p. 423.

fied and comforted." [13]   Undoubtedly, the multitudes who heard Elias Hicks preach in 1828 went away wondering what all the trouble was about.

Elias and his traveling companion reached home about the middle of First month, 1829.   This was one of the longest and most extended religious journeys ever made by him, and was completed within two months of his eighty-first year.   On the journey he traveled nearly 2400 miles, and was absent seven months and ten days.

Going carefully over the various journeys of this well-known minister, a conservative estimate will show that he traveled in the aggregate not less than forty thousand miles during his long life of public service.   He was probably the best-known minister in the Society of Friends in his time.   His circle of personal friends was large, and extended over all the yearly meetings.   It is necessary to keep these facts in mind, in order to understand how the major portion of Friends at that time made his cause their own when the rupture came.

The majority of Friends at that time were content as to preaching, with words that seemed to be full of spirit and life, and this undoubtedly was characteristic of the preaching of Elias Hicks.   To attempt to destroy the standing in the Society of a man of such character and equipment was certain to break something other than the man attacked.   This will become more apparent as we consider more closely the relation of Elias Hicks to the controversy with which his name and person were linked, and with the trouble in the Society of Friends, for which, either justly or otherwise, he was made the scapegoat.

---

[13] Journal, p. 423.

THE HICKS' HOUSE, JERICHO.
(See page 66.)

FRIENDS' MEETING HOUSE, JERICHO.
(See page 68.)

CHAPTER VII.

Ideas About the Ministry.

To CONSTRUCT from the published deliverances, and personal correspondence of Elias Hicks, a statement of his theory and practice touching the ministry is desirable if not easy. That he considered public religious exercise an exalted function, if of the right sort, and emanating from the Divine source, is abundantly evidenced in all he said and wrote. The call to particular and general service, whether in his home meeting for worship, or in connection with his extended religious journeys, he believed came directly from the Divine Spirit.

One instance is related, which possibly as clearly as anything, illustrates his feeling regarding the ministry, and the relationship of the Infinite to the minister. In the fall of 1781, when his service in the ministry had been acknowledged about three years, he was very ill with a fever, which lasted for several months. In the most severe period of this indisposition he tells us that "a prospect opened to my mind to pay a religious visit to some parts of our island where no Friends lived, and among a people, who, from acquaintance I had with them, were more likely to mock than receive me." He opposed the call, and argued against it, only to see the disease daily reducing his bodily and mental strength. He became convinced that in yielding to this call lay his only hope of recovery, and had he not done so his life would have gone out. Having fully recovered, the intimated service was performed the following summer.

He seemed to treat his ministry as something in a measure apart from his personality. He repeatedly referred

8

to his own ministerial labors in a way not unlike that indulged in by his most ardent admirers. Yet this was always accompanied with acknowledgment of the Divine enlightening and assistance. On the 22d of Tenth month, 1779, he held an appointed meeting in Hartford, Conn., a thousand persons being present. Of this meeting he said: "The Lord, in whom we trust, was graciously near, and furnished us with ability to conduct the meeting to the satisfaction and peace of our own minds; and to the edification of many present, and general satisfaction to the assembly." [1]

Speaking of a meeting at Market Street, Philadelphia, in Fourth month, 1801, he remarked: "My spirit was set at liberty, and ability afforded to divide the word among them, according to their varied conditions, in a large, searching and effectual testimony; whereby a holy solemnity was witnessed to spread over the meeting, to the great rejoicing of the honest-hearted." [2]

At a meeting at Goose Creek, Virginia, the 22d of Third month, 1797, he tells us: "After a considerable time of silent labor, in deep baptism with the suffering seed, my mouth was opened in a clear, full testimony, directed to the states of those present. And many were brought under the influence of that power which 'cut Rahab, and wounded the dragon.'" [3]

In the acknowledgment of the Divine influence and favor, Elias Hicks had a collection of phrases which he repeatedly used. "It was the Lord's doings, and marvelous in our eyes," was a common expression. He repeatedly said: "Our sufficiency was not of ourselves, but of God; and that the Lord was our strength from day to day, who

---

[1] Journal, p. 85.

[2] Journal, p. 89.

[3] Journal, p. 69.

is over all blessed forever." One of his favorite expressions was: "To the Lord be all the praise, nothing due to man."

Trite and pointed Scripture quotations were always at command, and they were effectively employed, both in speaking and writing. It will be noted by the reader that not a few of the expressions used by Elias Hicks sound like the phrases coined by George Fox.

That Elias Hicks believed in the plenary inspiration of the preacher is well attested. His testimony was constantly against the "letter," with little recognition that the letter could ever contain the spirit. Here is a sample exhortation to ministers:

"And it is a great thing when ministers keep in remembrance that necessary caution of the divine Master, not to premeditate what they shall say; but carefully to wait in the nothingness and emptiness of self, that what they speak may be only what the Holy Spirit speaketh in them; then will they not only speak the truth, but the truth, accompanied with power, and thereby profit the hearers."[4]

He admonished Friends in meeting, and especially ministers, to "get inward, and wait in their proper gifts." The evident theory was that by waiting, and possibly wrestling with the manifestation it was possible to tell whether it was from below or above.

Still, there was not an entire absence of the human and even the rational in Elias Hicks' theory of the ministry as it worked out in practice. He had evidently discovered the psychological side of public speaking to the extent of recognizing that even the preacher was influenced by his audience.

When he was in Philadelphia in 1816, before the

---

4 Journal, p. 296.

troubled times had arrived, he tells us that "it proved a
hard trying season: one of them [ministers] was exercised
in public testimony, and although she appeared to labor fer-
vently, yet but little life was felt to arise during the meeting.
This makes the work hard for the poor exercised ministers,
who feel the necessity publicly to advocate the cause of truth
and righteousness, and yet obtain but little relief, by reason
of the deadness and indifference of those to whom they are
constrained to minister. I found it my place to sit silent
and suffer with the seed." [5]

In a personal letter, while on one of his visits, Elias
Hicks gave the following impression of the meeting and the
ministry:

"To-day was the quarterly meeting of discipline. It
was large, and I think in the main a favored instructive
season, although considerably hurt by a pretty long, tedious
communication, not sufficiently clothed with life to make
it either comfortable or useful. So it is, the Society is in
such a mixed and unstable state, and many who presume
to be teachers in it, are so far from keeping on the original
foundation, the light and spirit of truth, and so built up in
mere tradition, that I fear a very great portion of the
ministry among us, is doing more harm than good, and
leading back to the weak and beggarly elements, to which
they seem desirous to be again in bondage." [6]

This is not the only case of his measuring the general
effect of the ministry. In Seventh month, 1815, he attended
Westbury Quarterly Meeting, and of its experiences he
wrote as follows:

"Was the parting meeting held for public worship. It
was a large crowded meeting, but was somewhat hurt in
the forepart, by the appearance of one young in the ministry
standing too long, and manifesting too much affectation:

[5] Journal, p. 271.

[6] Letter to his wife, dated Purchase, N. Y., Tenth month 29, 1823.

Yet, I believed, he was under the preparing hand, fitting
for service in the Church, if he only keeps low and humble,
and does not aspire above his gift, into the animation of the
creature. For there is great danger, if such are not deeply
watchful, of the transformer getting in and raising the mind
into too much creaturely zeal, and warmth of the animal
spirit, whereby they may be deceived, and attribute that
to the divine power, which only arises from a heated imagination, and the natural warmth of their own spirits; and
so mar the work of the divine spirit on their minds, run
before their gift and lose it, or have it taken away from
them. They thereby fall into the condition of some formerly, as mentioned by the prophet, who, in their creaturely zeal, kindle a fire of their own, and walk in the light
thereof; but these, in the end, have to lie down in sorrow." [7]

Of the same quarterly meeting, held in Fourth month
in the following year, in New York, Elias wrote: "It was
for the most part a favored season, but would have been
more so, had not some in the ministry quite exceeded the
mark by unnecessary communication. For very great care
ought to rest on the minds of ministers, lest they become
burthensome, and take away the life from the meeting, and
bring over it a gloom of death and darkness, that may be
sensibly felt." [8]

His feeling regarding his own particular labor in the
ministry is almost pathetically expressed as follows:

"Meetings are generally large and well-attended, although in the midst of harvest. I have continual cause for
deep humility and thankfulness of heart under a daily sense
of the continued mercy of the Shepherd of Israel, who when
he puts his servants forth, goes before them, and points out
the way, when to them all seems shut up in darkness.
This has been abundantly my lot from day to day, insomuch
that the saying of the prophet has been verified in my experience, that none are so blind as the Lord's servants, nor

[7] Journal, p. 234.

[8] Journal, p. 268.

deaf as his messengers. As generally when I first enter
meetings I feel like one, both dumb and deaf, and see nothing but my own impotence. Nevertheless as my whole
trust and confidence is in the never-failing arm of divine
sufficiency, although I am thus emptied, I am not cast
down, neither has a murmuring thought been permitted to
enter, but in faith and patience, have had to inherit the
promise, as made to Israel formerly by the prophet. 'I will
never leave thee, nor forsake thee.' This my dear, I trust
will be the happy lot of all those who sincerely trust in the
Lord, and do not cast away their confidence, nor lean to
their own understanding." [9]

Occasionally in his ministry Elias Hicks did what in
our time would be called sensational things. In this matter
he shall be his own witness. Fourth-day, the 6th of
Twelfth month, 1815, at Pearl Street meeting in New York,
there was a marriage during the meeting, on which account
the attendance was large. After remarking that his mind
was "exercised in an unusual manner," he says:

"For the subject which first presented, after my mind
had become silenced, was the remembrance of the manner
in which the temporal courts among men are called to
order; and it became so impressive, as to apprehend it
right to make use of it as a simile, much in the way the
prophet was led to make use of some of the Recabites, to
convict Israel of their disobedience and want of attention to
their law and law-giver. I accordingly was led to cry
audibly three times, 'O yes! O yes! O yes! silence all persons, under the pain and penalty of the displeasure of the
court.' This unusual address had a powerful tendency to
arrest the attention of all present, and from which I took
occasion, as truth opened the way, to reason with the assembly, that if such a confused mass of people as are
generally collected together on such occasions, and from
very different motives, and many from mere curiosity to
hear and see the transactions of the court, should all in
an instant so honor and respect the court, as immediately

---

[9] Letter to his wife, written from East Caln, Pa., Seventh month
22, 1813.

to be still and silent at the simple call of the crier: How
much more reasonable is it, for a collection of people,
promiscuously gathered to the place appointed in a religious
way, to wait upon, and worship the Judge of heaven and
earth, to be still, and strive to silence every selfish and
creaturely thought and cogitation of the mind. For such
thoughts and cogitations would as certainly prevent our
hearing the inward divine voice of the King of heaven, and
as effectually hinder our worshipping him in spirit and in
truth, as the talking of the multitude at a court of moral
law, would interrupt the business thereof. As I proceeded
with this simile, the subject enlarged and spread, accompanied with gospel power and the evident demonstration of
the spirit, whereby truth was raised into victory, and ran
as oil over all. The meeting closed with solemn supplica-
tion and thanksgiving to the Lord our gracious Helper, to
whom all the honor and glory belong, both now and forever." [10]

Whatever may have been the opinion of Elias Hicks
as to the inspiration of the minister, he evidently did not
consider that it was so impersonal and accidental, or so
entirely outside the preacher, as to demand no care on his
own part. The following advisory statement almost provides for what might be called "preparation:"

"In those large meetings, where Friends are collected
from various parts, the weak and the strong together, and
especially in those for worship, it is essentially necessary
that Friends get inward, and wait in their proper gifts,
keeping in view their standing and place in society, especially those in the ministry. For otherwise there is danger
even from a desire to do good, of being caught with the
enemies' transformations, particularly with those that are
young, and inexperienced; for we seldom sit in meetings but
some prospect presents, which has a likeness, in its first
impression, to the right thing; and as these feel naturally
fearful of speaking in large meetings, and in the presence
of their elderly friends, and apprehending they are likely to
have something to offer, they are suddenly struck with the

fear of man, and thereby prevented from centering down
to their gifts, so as to discover whether it is a right motion
or not; and the accuser of the brethren, who is always
ready with his transformations to deceive, charges with
unfaithfulness and disobedience, by which they are driven
to act without any clear prospect, and find little to say, except making an apology for their thus standing; by which
they often disturb the meeting, and prevent others, who
are rightly called to the work, and thereby wound the
minds of the living baptized members." [11]

The responsibility which Elias Hicks felt for the meeting of which he was a member, and in which he felt called
to minister, is well illustrated in the following quotation:

"I was under considerable bodily indisposition most
of this week. On Fifth-day, so much so, as almost to give
up the prospect of getting to meeting; but I put on my
usual resolution and went, and was glad in so doing, as
there I met with that peace of God that passeth all understanding, which is only known by being felt. I had to declare to my friends how good it is to trust in the Lord with
all the heart, and lean not to our own understandings, lest
they fail us." [12]

This records no uncommon occurrence. He was often
indisposed, but the illness had to be severe if it kept him
away from meeting.

During his later life he was frequently indisposed, and
sometimes under such bodily pain when speaking that he
was forced to stop in the midst of a discourse. This
happened in Green Street Meeting House, Philadelphia,
Eleventh month 12, 1826. On this occasion the stenographer says that after "leaving his place for a few minutes,
he resumed." During this particular sermon Elias sat down
twice, beside the time mentioned, evidently to recover physi-
cal strength.

---

[11] Journal, p. 230.

[12] Journal, p. 230.

Elias Hicks was not one of those ministers who always spoke if he attended meeting. Many times he was silent; this being especially true when in his home meeting. When on a religious visit he generally spoke, but not always. That his willingness to "famish the people from words," tended to his local popularity, is quite certain.

The printed sermons of Elias Hicks would indicate that at times he was quite lengthy, and seldom preached what is known now as a short, ten-minute sermon. Estimating a number of sermons, we find that they averaged about 6500 words, so that his sermons must have generally occupied from thirty to forty-five minutes in delivery. Occasionally a sermon contained over 8000 words, while sometimes less than 4000 words.

CHAPTER VIII.

The Home at Jericho.

THE village of Jericho, Long Island, is about 25 miles east of New York City, in the town of Oyster Bay. It has had no considerable growth since the days of Elias Hicks, and now contains only about a score and a half of houses. Hicksville, less than two miles away, the railroad station for the older hamlet, contains a population of a couple of thousand. It was named for Valentine Hicks, the son-in-law of Elias.

Running through Jericho is the main-traveled road from the eastern part of Long Island to New York, called Jericho Pike. In our time it is a famous thoroughfare for automobiles, is thoroughly modern, and as smooth and hard as a barn floor. In former days it was a toll-road, and over it Elias Hicks often traveled. A cross-country road runs through Jericho nearly north and south, leading to Oyster Bay. On this road, a few rods to the north from the turn in the Jericho Pike stands the house which was originally the Seaman homestead, where Elias Hicks lived from soon after his marriage till his death.

The house was large and commodious for its time, but has been remodeled, so that only part of the building now standing is as it was eighty years ago. The house ends to the road, with entrance from the south side. It was of the popular Long Island and New England construction, shingled from cellar wall to ridge-pole. Four rooms on the east end of the house, two upstairs and two down, are practically as they were in the days of Elias Hicks. In one of these he had his paralytic stroke, and in another he passed away. The comparatively wide hall which runs across the house, with the exception of the stairway, is as it was in the time of its distinguished occupant. A new stairway of modern construction now occupies the opposite side of the hall from the one of the older time. This hall-way, it is said, Elias Hicks loved to promenade, sometimes with his visitors, and here with characteristic warmth of feeling he sped his parting guests, when the time for their departure came.

Like the most of his neighbors, Elias Hicks was a farmer. The home place probably contained about seventy-five acres, but he possessed detached pieces of land, part of it in timber. Several years before his death he sold forty acres of the farm to his son-in-law, Valentine Hicks, thus considerably reducing the care which advancing years and increased religious labor made advisable.

Jericho still retains its agricultural character more than some of the other sections of neighboring Long Island. The multi-millionaire and the real estate exploiter have absorbed many of the old Friendly homes toward the Westbury neighborhood, and are pushing their ambitious intent at land-grabbing down the Jericho road.

If Elias were to return and make a visit from Jericho to the meeting at Westbury, as he often did in his time, three or four miles away, he would pass more whizzing automobiles en route than he would teams, and would see the landscape beautifully adorned with lawns and walks, with parks and drives on the hillsides, not to mention the costly Roman garden of one of Pittsburg's captains of industry. Should he so elect, he could be whirled in a gasoline car in a few minutes over a distance which it probably took him the better part of an hour to make in his day. As he went along he could muse over snatches of

Goldsmith's "Deserted Village," like the following, which would be approximately, if not literally, true:

"Hoards, e'en beyond the miser's wish abound,
And rich men flock from all the world around.
Yet count our gains: this wealth is but a name
That leaves our useful products just the same.
And so the loss: the man of wealth and pride
Takes up the place that many poor supplied;
Space for his lake, his parks extending bounds,
Space for his horses, equipage and hounds,   -
The robe that wraps his limbs in silken sloth,
Has robbed the neighboring fields of half their growth."

But there are some compensations in the modern scene, and however emotionally sad the change, the helpfully suggestive side is not in lamentation over the inevitable, but in considering the growing demands which the situation makes upon the practical spiritual religion which Elias Hicks preached, and in which his successors still profess to believe.

A hundred years ago, wheat was a regular and staple farm product on Long Island, especially in and around Jericho, and on the Hicks farm. But no wheat is raised in this section now. The farmer finds it more profitable to raise the more perishable vegetables to feed the hungry hordes of the great city, which has crowded itself nearer and nearer to the farmers' domain.

Less than a quarter of a mile up the road from the Hicks home is the Friends' Meeting House, which Elias Hicks helped to build, if he did not design it. The timbers and rafters, which were large, and are still sound to the core, were hewed by hand of course. Like most of the neighboring buildings, its sides were shingled, and probably the original shingles have not been replaced since the house was built, a hundred and twenty-two years ago. The "public gallery" contained benches sloping steeply one above the other, making the view of the preacher's gallery easy from these elevated positions. Over the preacher's gallery, and facing the one just described, is room for a row of seats behind a railing. Whether this was a sort of a "watch-tower" from which the elders might observe the deportment of the young people in the seats opposite, or whether it was simply used for overflow purposes, tradition does not tell us.

The fact probably is that what is known as the Hicks property at Jericho came to Elias by his wife Jemima. There is every reason to believe that at the time of his marriage he was a poor man, and as the young folks took up their residence at the Seaman home soon after their marriage, there was no time for an accumulation of property on the part of the head of the new family. The economic situation involved in the matter under consideration had a most important bearing on the religious service of Elias Hicks. Taking the Seaman farm brought him economic certainty, if not independence. It is hardly conceivable that he could have given the large attention to the "free gospel ministry" which he did, had there been a struggle with debt and difficulty which was so incidental in laying the foundations of even a moderate success a century and a quarter ago. It is by no means to be inferred, however, that Elias Hicks was ever a wealthy man, or possessed the means of luxury, for which of course he had no desire, and against which he bore a life-long testimony. The real point to be gratefully remembered is that he was not overburdened with the care and worry which a less desirable economic condition would have enforced.

In the main, Elias Hicks saw his married children settle around him. Royal Aldrich, who married his oldest daughter, had a tannery, and lived on the opposite side of the road not far away. Valentine Hicks, who married another daughter, had a somewhat pretentious house for the time, at the foot of the little hill approaching the meeting house, and just beyond the house of Elias, Robert Seaman, who married the youngest daughter, lived only a few steps away. Joshua Willets, who married the third daughter, resided on the south side of the island, some miles distant. The time of scattering families, lured by business outlook and economic advantage, had not yet arrived.

CHAPTER IX.

The Hicks Family.

IN THE home at Jericho the children of Elias Hicks were born. Touching his family we have this bit of interesting information from Elias Hicks himself:

"My wife, although not of a very strong constitution, lived to be the mother of eleven children, four sons and seven daughters. Our second daughter, a very lovely promising child, died when young with the small pox, and the youngest was not living at its birth. The rest all arrived to years of discretion, and afforded us considerable comfort, as they proved to be in a good degree. dutiful children. All our sons, however, were of weak constitutions, and were not able to take care of themselves, being so enfeebled as not to be able to walk after the ninth year of their age. The two eldest died in the fifteenth year of their age, the third in his seventeenth year, and the youngest was nearly nineteen when he died. But, although thus helpless, the innocency of their lives, and the resigned cheerfulness of their dispositions to their allotments, made the labour and toil of taking care of them agreeable and pleasant; and I trust we were preserved from murmuring or repining, believing the dispensation to be in wisdom, and according to the will and gracious disposing of an all-wise providence, for purposes best known to himself. And when I have observed the great anxiety and affliction, which many parents have with undutiful children who are favoured with health, especially their sons, I could perceive very few whose troubles and exercises, on that account, did not far exceed ours. The weakness and bodily infirmity of our sons tended to keep them much out of the way of the troubles and temptations of the world; and we believed that in their death they were happy, and admitted into the realms of peace and joy; a reflection, the most comfortable and joyous that parents can have in regard to their tender offspring." [1]

The children thus referred to by their father were the following: Martha, born in 1771. She married Royal Aldrich, and died in 1862, at the advanced age of ninety-one. She was a widow for about twenty years.

David was born in 1773, and died in 1787. Elias, the second son, was born in 1774, and died the same year as his brother David. Elizabeth was born in 1777, and died in 1779. This is the daughter who had the small pox. There are no records telling whether the other members of the family had the disease, or how this child of two years became a victim of the contagion.

Phebe, the third daughter, was born in 1779. She married Joshua Willets, as noted in the last chapter.

Abigail, who married Valentine Hicks, a nephew of Elias, was born in 1782. She died Second month 26, 1850, while her husband passed away the 5th of Third month of the same year, just one week after the death of his wife

Jonathan, the third son, was born in 1784, and passed away in 1802. His brother, John, was born in 1789, and died in 1805.

Elizabeth, evidently named for her little sister, was born in 1791, and lived to a good old age. She passed away in 1781. She was never married, and occasionally accompanied her father on his religious visits. She was known in the neighborhood, in her later years at least, as "Aunt Elizabeth," and is the best-remembered of any of the children of Elias Hicks. As the Friends remember her she was a spare woman, never weighing over ninety pounds.

The youngest child of the family, Sarah, was born in

---

[1] Journal, p. 14.

1793. She married Robert Seaman, her kinsman, and died in 1835. Robert, her husband, died in 1860.

It will be seen that the home at Jericho was a house acquainted with grief. Of the ten children, Martha, David, Elias and little Elizabeth made up the juvenile members of the household, up to the time of the death of the latter, Phebe came the same year, while Abigail was born three years later, so that there were at least four or five children always gathered around the family board. Before the passing away of Elias and David, the family had been increased by the birth of Jonathan, making the children living at one time six. After the death of the three older boys, and the birth of Elizabeth and Sarah, until the death of John in 1805, the living children were still six in number. The five daughters, Martha, Phebe, Abigail, Elizabeth and Sarah all outlived their parents.

Elias Hicks was undoubtedly a most affectionate father, as the letters to his wife and children show. How much this was diluted by the apparent sternness of his religious concerns is a matter for the imagination to determine. What were the amusements of this large family is an interesting question in this "age of the child," with its surfeit of toys and games. What were the tasks of the girls it is not so hard to answer. Of course they worked "samplers," pieced quilts, learned to spin and knit, and possibly to weave, and to prepare the wool or flax for the loom. If we read between the lines in the description of their father, we can easily infer that the physically afflicted sons were nevertheless not without the joys of boyhood.

At all events, if it was an afflicted family, it was also a united one. It was a home where the parents were reverenced by the children, and where there was a feeling of love, and a sense of loyalty. This feeling is still character-

10

istic of the descendants of Elias Hicks. It is a sample of
the persistence of the qualities of a strong man, in the generations that come after him.

Of the four daughters of Elias Hicks who were
married, but two had children, so that the lineal descendants
of the celebrated Jericho preacher are either descendants of
Martha Hicks, wife of Valentine, or of Sarah Hicks Seaman. These two branches of the family are quite
numerous. [2]

Of Jemima, the wife of Elias Hicks, little is known
apart from the correspondence of her husband, and that is
considerable. That he considered her his real help-meet,
and had for her a lover's affection to the end is abundantly
attested by all of the facts. Dame Rumor, in the region of
Jericho, claims that she was her husband's intellectual in-
ferior, but that is an indefinite comparison worth very little.
That she was at some points his superior is undoubtedly
true, and it must be remembered that Elias himself, with all
of his great natural ability, lacked intellectual culture and
literary training. Jemima was evidently a good house-
keeper, and manager of affairs. Before she had sons-in-
law with whom to advise, and even after that, the business
side of the family was a considerable part of the time in her
hands. It is no small matter to throw upon a woman,
never robust, the responsibility of both the mother and
father of a family during the prolonged absence of the
husband.

The first long religious visit of Elias Hicks lasted ten
weeks. At that time there were four little people in the
Hicks home, from eight-year-old Martha to two-year-old
Elizabeth, who died that year, while Phebe was born after
the return of her father from his Philadelphia trip. Sev-

---

[2] The descendants referred to will be given in their proper place
in the Appendix.

eral of the other extended journeys were made while the children of the family were of an age requiring care. Of course this laid labor and responsibility on the wife and mother. These she bore without complaining and, we may be sure, with executive ability of no mean order.

It was a time when women were not expected to be either the intellectual peers or companions of their husbands, and we cannot justly apply the measurements and standards of to-day, to the women of a century ago. Men of the Elias Hicks type, meeting their fellows in public assemblies and ministering to them, traveling widely and forming many friendships, whether in the Society of Friends or out of it, are likely to be praised, if not petted, while their wives, less known, labor on unappreciated. Such a woman was Jemima Hicks. To her, and all like her, the lasting gratitude of the sons of men is due.

CHAPTER X.

Letters to his Wife.

In the long absences from home, which the religious visits of Elias Hicks involved, as a matter of course many of the domestic burdens fell heavily upon his wife. In so far as he could atone for his absence by sending epistles home he did so. In fact, for the times, he was a voluminous letter writer.

It was not a time of rapid transit. Distances now spanned in a few hours demanded days and weeks when Elias Hicks was active in the ministry. At the best, but a few letters could reach home from the traveler absent for several months.

In the main the letters which Elias sent to his beloved Jemima were of the ardent lover-like sort. It seemed impossible, however, for him to avoid the preacherly function in even his most tender and domestic missives. Exhortations to practical righteousness, and to the maintenance of what he considered the Friendly fundamentals, were plentifully mixed with his most private and personal concerns.

In going over this correspondence one wishes for more discription, relating to the human side of the traveler's experiences. A man who several times traversed what was really the width of habitable America, and mostly either in a wagon or on horseback, must have seen much that was interesting, and many times humorous and even pathetic. But few of these things moved Elias Hicks, or diverted him from what he considered the purely gospel character of his mission.

Still there is much worth while in this domestic correspondence. From it we compile and annotate such extracts as seem to help reveal the character of the man who wrote them.

On the 13th of Eighth month, 1788, Elias was at Creek, now Clinton Corners, in Dutchess county, New York. From a letter written to his wife that day, we quote:

"My heart glows at this time with much love and affection for thee and our dear children, with breathing desires for your preservation, and that thou, my dear, may be kept in a state of due watchfulness over thyself, and those dear lambs under thy care, that nothing may interrupt the current of pure love among you in my absence."

A letter dated "Lynn, Massachusetts, ye 24th of eighth month, 1793," and written to his wife, is of peculiar interest. We quote the first sentences:

"I received last evening, at my return to this place from the East, thy very acceptable letter of the 16th instant. . . . The contents, except the account of the pain in thy side, were truly comfortable. That part wherein thou expresseth a resignation to the Divine Will, was particularly satisfactory, for in this, my dear, consists our chiefest happiness and consolation."

He sometimes expressed a sense of loneliness in his travels, but was certain of the nearness of the Divine Spirit. In the letter mentioned above he said:

"Thou hast cause to believe with me, my dear, that it was He that first united our hearts together in the bonds of an endeared love and affection. So it is He that has kept and preserved us all our life long, and hath caused us to witness an increase of that unfading love, which as thou expresseth is ever new."

Evidently his beloved Jemima, like Martha of old, was unduly troubled about many things, for we find Elias in his letter indulging in the following warning: "And let me again hint to thee a care over thyself, for I fear thou wilt expose thyself by too much bodily exercise in the care of thy business."

It is seldom that we find even a tinge of complaining in any of his letters. It seems, however, that his women folks were not industrious correspondents. In closing the letter noted he thus expressed himself:

"My companion receives his packet of letters, frequently four, five or six at a time, which makes me feel as if I was forgotten by my friends, having received but two small letters from home since I left you. And thou writest, my dear, as if paper was scarce, on very small pieces."

On the 3d of Ninth month, of the same year, a letter was written to his wife, much like the foregoing. It is interesting to note that Elias was at this time the guest of Moses Brown (in Providence), the founder of the Moses Brown School. The small pieces of paper mentioned are hints of a wifely economy, not altogether approved by her very economical husband. There is a gentle tinge of rebuke in the following, written from Nine Partners, Eleventh month 19, 1818. The temptation is strong to read into these lines, a grain of humor touching the much-talked-of persistence of a woman's will:

"Inasmuch as I have often felt concerned when thus absent, least thou should worry thyself, with too much care and labor in regard to our temporal concerns, and have often desired thee to be careful in that respect, but mostly without effect, by reason that thou art so choice of thy own free agency as to be afraid to take the advice of thy best friend, lest it might mar that great privilege; I therefore now propose to leave thee at full liberty to use it in thine own pleasure with the addition of this desire, that thou use it in that way as will produce to thee the most true comfort and joy, and then I trust I shall be comforted, my dear, in thy comfort, and joyful in thy joy."

A letter dated West Jersey, near Salem, the 6th of First

month, 1798, mentions a singular concern about apparel. He exhorts his wife to guard the tender minds of their children from "foolish and worldly vanities," and then drops into a personal and general statement regarding what he considered simplicity and plainness as follows:

"Great is the apparent departure from primitive purity and plainness among many professors of the truth, where our lots have been cast. Foreseeing that I may often be led in a line of close doctrine to such it has brought me under close self-examination, knowing for certain that those who have to deal out to others ought to look well to their own going. In this time of scrutiny nothing turned up as bringing reproof to my mind concerning our children, but the manner of wearing their gown sleeves long and pinned at the wrist. This I found to strike at the pure life, and wounded my mind. I clearly saw my deficiency that I had not more endeavored to have it done away with before I left home, for I felt it as a burden then. But seeing our dear daughters had manifested so much condescension in other things, and this being like one of the least, I endeavored to be easy under it. But feeling it with assurance not to be a plant of our Heavenly Father's right-hand planting, think it ought to be plucked up. Let our dear daughters read these lines, and tell them their dear father prays they may wisely consider the matter, and if they can be willing so far to condescend to my desire while absent as to have these things removed, it will be as balsam to my wounded spirit, and they will not go without their reward. But their father's God will bless them and become their God, as they are faithful to his reproofs in their hearts, and walk fearfully before Him. He will redeem them, out of all adversity to the praise and glory of His grace, who is over all, God, blessed forever."

During a visit to Nine Partners, Twelfth month 15, 1803, Elias wrote to Jemima. Evidently she had repelled the inference, if not the implication, that she had been negligent in her correspondence, for we find the letter in question beginning in this fashion:

"Although I wrote thee pretty fully last evening, yet having since that received a precious, refreshing letter from thee, by Isaac Frost (it being the first I have received from thee since I left home), but finding from thy last that thou hast written several. It affords a singular satisfaction in finding thou hast been mindful of me. But I have not complained, my dear, nor let in, nor indulged a thought that thou hadst forgotten me, nor do I believe thou couldst. There is nothing while we continue in our right minds that can dissolve that firm and precious bond of love and endeared affection, which from our first acquaintance united us together, and in which, while writing these lines my spirit greets thee with endeared embraces."

It surely seems strange that a man who was the father of eleven children, that his only source of personal "reproof" concerning them, was this little matter of the sleeves and the pins. This probably is a fair illustration of what may be called the conservatism of Elias Hicks touching all of the peculiarities of the Society of Friends.

The postscript to a letter written to Jemima from Shrewsbury, New Jersey, Twelfth month 17, 1797, reads as follows: "As thou writes but poorly, if thou should get Hallet or Royal to write superscriptions on the letters, it would make them more plain for conveyance."

It was only seldom that business affairs at home were referred to in his epistles to his wife. But occasionally a departure was made from this practice. Where these lapses do occur, it would seem that they should be noted. In the fall of 1822 Elias was in the vicinity of Philadelphia, and was stopping with his friend and kinsman, Edward Hicks, at Newtown, in Bucks county.

In this letter he says: "My health is much the same as when I left home. I was disappointed in not meeting any letters here, as I feel very anxious how you all do." We copy the balance of the letter, with its tender addition to Jemima:

"I will just remind thee that before I left home I put two old ewes in the green rye on the plains. If they should improve as to be fit to kill, I should be willing thou would let Josiah have one of them, as he agreed to split up some of the timber that was blown down in the woods by him, into rails and board himself. The other thou might sell or otherwise at thy pleasure.

"Now, my dear, let me remind thee of thy increasing bodily infirmities, and the necessity it lays thee under to spare thyself of the burthen and care of such bodily and mental labour and exercise, by which thou will experience more quiet rest, both to body and mind, and that it may be, my dear, our united care to endeavor that our last days may be our best days, that so we may witness a state and qualification to pass gently and quietly out of time, into the mansions of eternal blessedness, where all sighing and sorrow, will be at an end."

While in Pennsylvania, and at what is now York, Fourth month 3, 1798, he sent a tender missive home. Part of it referred to business matters. He gave directions for preparing the ground, and planting potatoes, and also for oats and flax, the latter being a crop practically unknown to present-day Long Island. He then gives the following direction regarding a financial obligation:

"And as James Carhartt has a bond of sixty pounds against me, of money belonging to a Dutchman, should be glad if thou hast not money enough by thee to pay the interest thereof, thou would call upon Royal or brother Joseph and get some, and pay it the first of Fifth month."

While at Rahway, New Jersey, Eleventh month 6, 1801, on his visit to Friends in New Jersey and Pennsylvania, he wrote one of his most expressive letters to Jemima. A postscript was attached directed to his daughters. To his oldest daughter, Martha, he sent an exhortation in which he said: "My desires for thee, my dear, are that thou may be preserved innocent and chaste to the Lord, for I can have no greater joy than to find my children walking in the truth."

That a large part of his concern was for the comfort

of his wife in the long absences from home is abundantly
shown in his entire correspondence. The last postscript to
the Railway letter is as follows:

"And, dear Phebe and Abigail, remember your Creator,
who made you not to spend your time in play and vanity,
but to be sober and to live in his fear, that he may bless
you. Be obedient to your dear mother, it is my charge to
you. Love and help her whatever you can; it will comfort your dear father."

The 2d of Eleventh month, 1820, Elias arrived at
Hudson, and learning that the steamboat to New York was
to pass that day, he prepared and sent a letter to his wife.
In this letter he says:

"It may be that some of my friends may think me so
far worth noticing, as to meet me with a line or two at Nine
Partners, as I have often felt very desirous of hearing how
you fare at home, but this desire hath mostly failed of
being gratified. I suppose the many things so absorb the
minds of my friends at home, that they have no time to
think of so poor a thing as I am. But never mind it, as
all things, it is said, will work together for good to those
that love and fear [God]."

While at Saratoga, in 1793, Elias wrote to Jemima.
Tenth month 15th. This is one of his most ardent epistles.
"Oh, my dear," he says, "may we ever keep in remembrance
the day of our espousal and gladness of our hearts, as I
believe it was a measure of the Divine Image that united our
hearts together in the beginning. It is the same that I believe has, and still doth strengthen the sweet, influential and
reciprocal bond, that nothing, I trust, as we dwell under a
sense of Divine love and in the pure fear, will ever be able
to obliterate or deface."

Third month 15, 1798, a letter was written from
Alexandria, Va., from which we take this extract:

"We came here this morning from Sandy Spring, which

is upwards of twenty miles distant. Got in timely so as to attend their meeting which began at the tenth hour. Crossed the river Potomac on our way. We got on horseback about break of day, and not being very well I thought I felt the most fatigued before I got in, I was ever sensible of before. When I came to the meeting, a poor little one it was, and wherein I had to suffer silence through the meeting for worship, but in their Preparative which followed, I found my way open in a measure to ease my mind."

CHAPTER XI.

The Slavery Question.

JOHN WOOLMAN was the mouth-piece of the best Quaker conscience of the eighteenth century on the slavery question. For twenty-five years before his death, in 1772, he was pleading with the tenderness of a woman that his beloved religious society should clear itself from complicity with the system which held human beings in bondage. His mantel apparently fell on Warner Mifflin, a young man residing in Kent county, Delaware, near the little hamlet of Camden. In 1775 Mifflin manumitted his slaves, and was followed by like conduct on the part of his father, Daniel Mifflin, a resident of Accomac County, in Virginia.

Warner Mifflin is said to have been the first man in America to voluntarily give freedom to his bondmen, and to make restitution to such of them as were past twenty-one, for the unrequited service which they had rendered him. Be that as it may, from 1775, until his death in 1799, Warner Mifflin, with tireless zeal labored with Friends personally, and with meetings in their official capacity, to drive the last remnant of slavery from the Quaker fold. His efforts appeared in various monthly meeting minutes throughout Philadelphia Yearly Meeting, and he was not backward in laying his concern before the Yearly Meeting itself. In 1783, on the initiative of Mifflin, the Yearly Meeting for Pennsylvania, New Jersey, Delaware and the Western Parts of Maryland and Virginia, memorialized the infant United States Congress in regard to slavery. The document was a striking one for the time, was signed in person by 535 Friends, and was presented to the Congress by a strong committee headed by Warner Mifflin.

These efforts at internal deliverance from connection and complicity with slavery produced speedy results, and before the close of the century not a Quaker slave holder remained in the Society, unless in some obscure cases that continued "under care." Having cleared its own skirts of slavery, the members of the Society became divided into two classes—the one anxious that the Quaker conscience should make its appeal to the general conscience for the entire abolition of the "great iniquity." The other class, satisfied with their own sinlessness in this particular, wished the Society to remain passive, and in no way mix with a public agitation of the mooted question. These two opposing views distracted the Society down to the very verge of the final issue in the slaveholders' rebellion.

Elias Hicks was three years Warner Mifflin's junior. He probably saw the Delaware abolitionist during his visits to Philadelphia Yearly Meeting before the death of Mifflin. Whether either ever saw or heard John Woolman cannot be positively stated. Mifflin was twenty-seven when the great New Jersey preacher and reformer passed away, and must have fallen under the spell of Woolman's inspiring leadership. Elias Hicks could hardly have escaped being influenced by this "elder brother," although he may never have seen him.

The subject of this biography was among those who believed that the Society of Friends had a message to the world along the line of its internal testimony against slavery, and he did not hesitate to deliver the message, though it disturbed the superficial ease in Zion. Still he had no definite plan apart from the appeal to conscience for settling the problem.

It must be remembered, however, that Elias Hicks passed away before the real abolition movement, as represented by Garrison and Phillips and their compeers, had begun its vigorous agitation, or organized its widely applied propaganda. What the attitude of Elias would have been toward Friends becoming members of the abolition societies, which after his death played such an important part, and touching which many Friends were either in doubt or in opposition we cannot even surmise.

Benjamin Lundy[1] commenced his literary warfare against slavery, with the ponderously named "Genius of Universal Emancipation," in 1821. Elias Hicks was one of Lundy's most concerned and faithful patrons, in some of his undertakings,[2] as appears in his personal correspondence.

The state of New York provided for the gradual emancipation of its slaves in 1799, so that Elias Hicks had to go away from home after that period to get into real slave territory. As has been seen he began bearing his testimony in meetings for worship against the institution in Maryland, where slave holding was the law of the land until the end.

There are statements more or less legendary to the effect that Elias was the owner of one slave, but of that there is no authentic evidence, while the probabilities are all against it. If he ever held a slave or slaves, he undoubtedly manumitted them. An act of such importance would hardly

---

[1] Benjamin Lundy was born of Quaker parents, First month 4, 1789, in Sussex County, New Jersey. He learned the trade of harness maker and saddler, and went to Ohio, where he became very much interested in the slavery question. In 1816 he issued an "Address" touching the evils of slavery. Of this Address, Horace Greely says, it contained the germ of the whole anti-slavery movement. In First month, 1821, he issued the first number of *The Genius of Universal Emancipation*. Lundy was interested in various schemes for colonization, and assisted many emancipated negroes to go to Hayti, and contemplated the establishment of a colony of colored people in Mexico. He died at Lowell, Illinois, Eighth month 22, 1839, and was buried in the Friends' burying ground at Clear Creek.

[2] Please inform Benjamin Lundy that I have procured fifty-two subscribers, or subscribers for fifty-two books, entitled, "Letters," etc.— Extract from letter to his son-in-law, Valentine Hicks, dated Jericho, Eleventh month 6, 1827.

have escaped record in the Journal, and no reference to it exists.

The controversies and disownments in the Society of Friends on account of the slavery question really came after the death of Elias. The trouble in New York resulting in the disownment of Isaac T. Hopper, James S. Gibbons and Charles Marriott came on more than a decade after his death. This entire controversy has been wrongly esti- mated by most of the biographers and historians, repre- senting the pronounced abolitionists of the period. It was not simply a contest between anti-slavery Friends and pro- slavery Friends. In fact the moving spirits against Isaac T. Hopper were not advocates or defenders of slavery as an institution. George F. White, who was probably the head and front of the move ment to disown Isaac T. Hopper, was not in favor of slavery. After his death his monthly meet- ing memorialized him, and among other things stated that he had for years refrained from using commodities made by slave labor.

The conservative wing of the Society was opposed to Friends becoming identified with any organization for any purpose outside of the Society. George F. White attacked temperance organizations, as he did abolition socie- ties.

It was a common inference, if not a claim, of the Garri- sonian abolitionists, that there were no real anti-slavery men outside of their organization. In Fifth month, 1840, there was a debate involving the abolition attitude of the Society of Friends in the town of Lynn, Massachusetts. In this debate William Lloyd Garrison said of the Society: "If it were an abolition society, its efforts would be identified with ours." [3]

---

[3] The "Liberator," May 1, 1841, P. 3.

In the same debate Oliver Johnson disputed the abolition claims of the Society of Friends, saying: "They have asserted for themselves the claim of being an abolition society. But we never could get into their meeting house." [4] Thus was the test of abolitionism made to hinge upon joining the Abolition Society.

That the attitude of the conservatives was ill-advised and reprehensible may be true. It is also true that this body of Friends were not in favor of any effort to overthrow slavery by popular agitation. They held that all other Christians should do what Friends had done, cease to hold slaves, and that would settle the whole question. However shortsighted this attitude may have been, very few, if any, of the Friends holding it, believed in holding black men in bondage. In fact it is pretty safe to assert that at no time after the Society had freed itself from direct complicity with slavery was there any considerable number of strictly pro-slavery Friends in this country.

In the disownments in the Society growing out of the slavery controversy there was never a direct charge of abolitionism brought against the accused. In Kennett Monthly Meeting in Chester County, Pa., where in about seven years thirty-four Friends were disowned, the charge was that the persons had "associated with others in forming, sustaining and supporting a professedly religious organization [5] distinct from and not owned by Friends, and have wholly declined attending our religious meetings." [6]

Of course, it is true that the Friends who took part in the Progressive Friends' movement were probably led to

---

[4] The "Liberator," May 1, 1841, p. 3.

[5] The "Progressive Friends."

[6] Records of Kennett Monthly Meeting, First month 6, 1857.

do so because the way did not open for them to be aggressively anti-slavery in the parent meeting.

The colonization scheme, that is a plan to colonize emancipated negroes either in Africa, or in Hayti, or elsewhere, was prominently urged during the time of Elias Hicks. Benjamin Lundy had a plan of this character which he attempted to make practical. Evan Lewis,[7] of New York, in 1820, was interested in an effort of this sort, and sought the advice of Elias Hicks in the matter.

We have not been able to find any reply to this particular letter, and are thus not warranted in saying whether Elias Hicks sympathized with such a scheme or not.

The attitude of Elias Hicks on the slavery question is only minutely referred to in his Journal. His private correspondence gives his feeling and conduct in the case, in not a few instances. From his general disposition one would expect to find his objections to slavery based entirely on moral and religious grounds. Still, evidence abounds that he had also considered the economic phases of the question, as note the following:

"I may further add that from forty years of observation that in all cases where opportunity has opened the way fairly to contrast the subject, it has afforded indubitable evidence to my mind, that free labor is cheaper and more profitable than that done by slaves."[8]

It seems to have been laid upon him to present the claims of the truth as he saw it, in slave-holding communities. He makes the following statement touching service of this kind in Virginia:

"I have passed through some proving seasons since I

[7] Evan Lewis, a New York Friend and business man. He corresponded with King Henry, of San Domingo. Was a warm friend of Elias Hicks, and after the "separation" wrote a pamphlet in defense of Elias.

[8] From letter written to James Cropper, of England, dated Baltimore, Eleventh month 2, 1822.   12

left Baltimore, in meetings where many negro masters attended, some of whom held fifty, some an hundred, and some it was thought one hundred and fifty of these poor people in slavery. Was led to treat on the subject in divers meetings, in such a manner and so fully to expose the iniquity and unrighteousness thereof, that some who had stouted* it out hitherto against all conviction, were much humbled and brought to a state of contrition, and not one individual had power to make any opposition. But truth reigned triumphantly over all, to the rejoicing of many hearts." [10]

Elias Hicks wrote a number of articles on the slavery question, and some of them were printed and publicly circulated. A letter written at Manchester, England, Seventh month 5, 1812, by Martha Routh, and addressed to Elias Hicks, says: "I have not forgot that I am debtor to thee this way, for two very acceptable and instructive epistles, the latter with a pamphlet setting forth the deep exercise of thy mind, and endeavors for the more full relief of our fellow-brethren, the African race." This letter informs Elias that the author sent his pamphlet to Thomas Clarkson.

Considerable was written by Elias Hicks on the slave trade, some of it existing as unpublished manuscript. An article, filling four closely written pages of foolscap, is among his literary effects. A very long letter was written to James Cropper, of England, on the same subject. Both of these documents were written while the slave-trade bill was pending in the British Parliament. Elias considered the measure entirely inadequate, holding that the domestic production of slaves was as inhuman and abhorrent, if not more so, as their importation from Africa. In the letter to Cropper this strong statement is found: "It ought ever to

---

* "Stouted" seems to have been a favorite word with Elias. He habitually uses it as representing an aggravated resistance to the truth.

[10] From letter written to his wife from Alexandria, Va., Third month 15, 1798.

be remembered that it is one of the most necessary and essential duties both towards God and man, for individuals and nations to exert all the power and influence they are possessed of, in every righteous and consistent way, to put an entire stop to all oppression, robbery and murder without partiality, as it respects nations or individuals."

Many times, in his published sermons, Elias Hicks dealt with the iniquity of slavery. Without doubt he expressed himself in like manner in sermons preached before interest in the man and his utterances caused his sermons to be stenographically reported and published.

"Oh! that our eyes might be opened, to see more deeply into the mystery of iniquity and godliness; that we might become conversant in godliness and so reject iniquity. For all this wicked oppression of the African race is of the mystery of iniquity. The man of sin and son of perdition does these works, and nothing else does them. Justice is fallen in the streets, and in the councils of the nation. How much justice there is; for they have it in their power to do justice to these poor oppressed creatures, but they are waiting till all their selfish notions are gratified." [11]

Elias Hicks was as strongly opposed to the lines of interest and economic conduct which indirectly supported slavery as he was to the institution itself. We quote:

"And for want of a sight of this oppression, how many there are who, though they seem not willing to put their hands upon a fellow creature to bind him in chains of bondage, yet they will do everything to help along by purchasing the labor of those poor creatures, which is like eating flesh and drinking blood of our poor fellow-creatures. Is it like coming home to justice? For the thief and oppressor are just alike; the one is as bad as the other." [12]

[11] From sermon preached at Newtown, Pa., Twelfth month 18, 1826. The "Quaker," Vol. 4, p. 183.
[12] From sermon preached at Abington, Pa., Twelfth month 15, 1826. The "Quaker," Vol. 4, p. 155.

In dealing with slavery and slaveholders, his language often bordered on what would now be called bitterness. Here is a case in point:

"Can slaveholders, mercenaries and hirelings, who look for their gain from this quarter, can they promote the religion of Jesus Christ? No, they are the cause of its reproach, for they are the cause of making unbelievers." [13]

His concern touching slavery was largely based on considerations of justice, and regard for the opportunity which he believed ought to be the right of all men. In one of his sermons he said:

"Thousands and tens of thousands have been forbidden the enjoyment of every good thing on earth, even of common school-learning; and must it still be so? God forbid it. But this would be a trifle, if they had the privilege of rational beings on the earth; that liberty which is the greatest of all blessings—the exercise of free agency. And here we are glutting ourselves with the toils of their labor! . . . But this noble testimony, of refusing to partake of the spoils of oppression, lies with the dearly beloved young people of this day. We can look for but little from the aged, who have been accustomed to these things." [14]

In the sermon "just referred to," we find the following:

"We are on a level with all the rest of God's creatures. We are not better for being white than others for being black; and we have no more right to oppress the blacks because they are black than they have to oppress us because we are white. Therefore, every one who oppresses his colored brother or sister is a tyrant upon the earth; and every one who strengthens the hand of an oppressor is a tyrant upon earth. They have turned from God, and have

---

[13] A series of extemporaneous discourses by Elias Hicks. Joseph and Edward Parker, p. 24.

[14] From sermon preached in Philadelphia, Twelfth month 1, 1824. Parker's "Discourses by Elias Hicks," p. 60-61.

not that powerful love, which does away all distinction and prejudice of education, and sets upon equal grounds all those that have equal rights." [15]

Of the "essays" on the slavery question written by Elias Hicks, one has survived, and is bound in the volume, "Letters of Elias Hicks." The pamphlet in question, though small, like many "ancient" productions, had a very large title, viz.: "Observations on the Slavery of the Africans and Their Descendants, and the Use of the Produce of Their Labor." [16] It was originally published in 1811, having been approved by the Meeting for Sufferings of New York Yearly Meeting. Nearly half of the "essay" is made up of a series of questions and answers. When printed it made six leaves the size of this page. On the subject of the product of slave labor, decided ground was taken, the claim being that all such produce was "prize goods." The reason for this claim was that the slaves originally were captives, practically the victims of a war of capture if not conquest. Among other things the essay argues the rightfulness and justice of any State to pass laws abolishing slavery within its borders.

While the arguments presented in this document are of general value, it is probable that the pamphlet was in the main intended for circulation among Friends, with a view to stimulating them to such action as would forward the cause of freedom. This essay by Elias Hicks antedated by five years the address by Benjamin Lundy, already referred to, and was probably one of the first publications in the nineteenth century actually advocating the abolition of slavery.

In studying the slavery question it is necessary to re-

---

[15] The same, p. 79.

[16] "Letters of Elias Hicks," p. 9.

member that before the invention of the cotton gin, about 1793, a considerable but unorganized and ineffective anti-slavery sentiment existed in the country. But after that invention, which rendered slave labor very remunerative, sentiment of this sort subsided so that the Friends, who, like Elias Hicks, advocated abolition during the first quarter of the nineteenth century, were really pioneers in the attempt which resulted in the freedom of a race.

At one time church organizations, even in the South, especially the Baptists, passed resolutions favorable to the abolition of slavery. Churches North and South in the decade between 1780 and 1790 were well abreast of Friends in this particular. Touching this latter Horace Greeley remarked: "But no similar declaration has been made by any Southern Baptist Convention since field-hands rose to $1,000 each, and black infants at birth were accounted worth $100." [17]

We could make copious extracts from the anti-slavery utterances of Elias Hicks, but our object is simply to give the scope of his thinking and purpose in regard to this matter. Few men at certain points were more altruistic than he, and as an altruist he could not do other than oppose the great social and economic iniquity of his time. From his standpoint slavery was utterly and irretrievably bad, and to bear testimony constant and consistent against it was part of the high calling of the Christian.

---

[17] "The American Conflict," by Horace Greeley, Vol. I p. 120.

CHAPTER XII.

Various Opinions.

ELIAS HICKS had very definite ideas on a great many subjects. While in many respects he was in advance of his time, at other points he was conservative. At any rate he was not in unity with some of the prevalent social and economic arrangements. On the question of property he entertained some startling convictions. Just how much public expression he gave to these views may not be positively determined. That he believed that there were grave spiritual dangers involved in getting and holding great wealth, is abundantly attested in his public utterances, but we must look to his private correspondence for some of his advanced views on the property question.

In a letter addressed to "Dear Alsop," dated Jericho, Fifth month 14, 1826, he deals quite definitely with the matter of property. After claiming that the early Christians wandered from the pure gospel of Jesus after they ceased to rely on the inward teacher, he makes a declaration on the subject as follows:

"But did we all as individuals take the spirit of truth, or light within, as our only rule and guide in all things, we should all then be willing, and thereby enabled, to do justly, love mercy, and walk humbly with God. Then we should hold all things in common, and call nothing our own, but consider all our blessings as only lent to us, to be used and distributed by us in such manner and way as his holy spirit, or this inward teacher, may from time to time direct. Hence we should be made all equal, accountable to none but God alone, for the right use or the abuse of his blessings. Then all mankind would be but one community, have but one head, but one father, and the saying of Jesus would be verified. We should no longer call any man master, for one only has a right to be our Master, even God, and all mankind become brethren. This is the kind of community that I have been labouring for more than forty years to introduce mankind into, that so we might all have but one head, and one instructor and he (God) come to rule whose only right it is, and which would always have been the case, had not man rebelled against his maker, and disobeyed his salutary instruction and commands."

Touching the "cares and deceitfulness of riches," he had much to say. He tells us that on a certain day he attended the meeting of ministers and elders in Westbury, and sat through it "under great depression and poverty of spirit." There was evidently some confession and not a little complaining, as there is now, regarding the possession and exercise of spiritual gifts on the part of Friends. But Elias affirmed that the "cloud" over the meeting was not "in consequence of a deficiency of ministers, as it respects their ministerial gifts, nor from a want of care in elders in watching over them; but from a much more deep and melancholy cause, viz.: the love and cares of this world and the deceitfulness of riches; which, springing up and gaining the ascendency in the mind, choke the good seed like the briars and thorns, and render it fruitless; and produce such great dearth and barrenness in our meetings." [1]

Elias Hicks apparently believed that labor had in itself a vital spiritual quality. In fact he held that the famous injunction in Genesis "In the sweat of thy face shalt thou eat bread" "was not a penalty, but it was a divine counsel— a counsel of perfect wisdom and perfect love." [2] It was his opinion that all oppression, slavery and injustice, had their origin in the disposition of men to shirk the obligation to

---

[1] Journal of Elias Hicks, p. 233.

[2] Sermon preached at Abington, Pa., Twelfth month 15, 1826. The "Quaker," p. 155.

CHILDREN OT ELIAS HICKS

Valentine Hicks (Son-in-Law)   Abigail Hicks

Martha Aldrich   Elizabeth Hicks

labor, thus placing burdens on their fellows, which they should bear themselves.

Every exhortation touching labor he religiously followed himself. He records that at the age of sixty he labored hard in his harvest field, and remarks with evident pride and satisfaction as follows:

"I found I could wield the scythe nearly as in the days of my youth. It was a day of thankful and delightful contemplation. My heart was filled with thankfulness and gratitude to the blessed Author of my existence, in a consideration of his providential care over me, in preserving me in health, and in the possession of my bodily powers, the exercise of which were still affording me both profit and delight; and I was doubly thankful for the continued exercise of my mental faculties, not only in instructing me how to exert and rightly employ my bodily powers, in the most useful and advantageous manner, but also in contemplating the works of nature and Providence, in the blessings and beauties of the field—a volume containing more delightful and profitable instruction than all the volumes of mere learning and science in the world.

"What a vast portion of the joys and comforts of life do the idle and slothful deprive themselves of, by running into cities and towns, to avoid labouring in the field; not considering that this is one of the principal sources that the gracious Creator of the universe has appointed to his creature, man, from whence he may derive great temporal happiness and delight. It also opens the largest and best field of exercise to the contemplative mind, by which it may be prepared to meet, when this mortal puts on immortality, those immortal joys that will ever be the lot of the faithful and industrious." [3]

It will probably be disputed in our time, that those who labor and attempt to live in cities enjoy lives of greater ease than those who till the soil.

While Elias recognized the obligation to labor, and believed it was a blessed privilege, he had learned in the school of experience that an over-worked body and an over-worried mind tended to spiritual poverty. We quote:

"The rest of this week was spent in my ordinary vocations. My farming business was very pressing, and it being difficult to procure suitable assistance, my mind was overburdened with care, which seldom fails of producing leanness of spirit in a lesser or greater degree." [4]

As offset to this we quote the following:

"What a favor it is for such an active creature as man, possessed of such powers of body and mind, always to have some employment, and something for those powers to act upon; for otherwise they would be useless and dormant, and afford neither profit nor delight." [5]

The building of railroads in this country had fairly begun when Elias Hicks passed away in 1830. Projects had been under way for some time, and certain Friends in Baltimore, then the center of railroad activity, had become interested in the enterprise. In a letter to Deborah and James P. Stabler, [6] written in New York, Sixth month 28, 1829, Elias expresses himself quite freely regarding the matter. He says: "It was a cause of sorrow rather than joy when last in Baltimore to find my dear friend P. E. Thomas [7] so

---

[4] Journal, p. 151.

[5] Journal, p. 184.

[6] Deborah Stabler was the widow of Dr. William Stabler, the latter being a brother of Edward Stabler, of Alexandria, the well-known preacher, and close friend of Elias Hicks. Deborah was a recorded minister. James P. was her son. He was chief engineer of the Baltimore and Susquehanna Railroad in its early construction, and was the first general superintendent and chief engineer of the Baltimore and Ohio, and built part of the line from Baltimore to Frederick. He was the author of a small pamphlet entitled, "The Certain Evidences of Practical Religion," published in 1884. He resided at Sandy Spring, Md.

[7] Philip E. Thomas, for many years sat at the head of the Baltimore meeting. He was the son of Evan Thomas, of Sandy Spring, who was a recorded minister. Philip E. was an importing hardware

fully engaged in that troublesome business of the railroad,[8] as I consider his calling to be of a more noble and exalted nature than to enlist in such low and groveling concerns. For it is a great truth that no man can serve two masters, for he will either love the one, and hate the other, or hold to the one, and despise the other. Ye cannot serve God and mammon. The railroad in this case I consider mammon."

The following is an extract from the same letter:

"It afforded me very pleasing sensations to be informed of dear James' improvement in health, but it excited some different feeling when informed that he had taken the place of Assistant Superintendent of the railroad company, a business. I conceive that principally belongs to the men of this world, but not to the children of light, whose kingdom is not of this world; for when we consider that there are thousands and tens of thousands who are voluntarily enlisted in works that relate to the accommodation of flesh and blood which can never inherit the kingdom of heaven."

The objection to railroads is one of those unaccountable but interesting contradictions which appear in the lives of some progressive men. By a sort of irony of fate, Valentine Hicks, the son-in-law of Elias, a few years after the death of the latter, became very much interested in the railroad business. The charter of the Long Island Railroad Company was granted Fourth month 24, 1834. In this document Valentine Hicks was named one of the commissioners to secure the capital stock, and appoint the first

---

merchant, a most successful business man, and the first president of the Baltimore and Ohio Railroad. In the construction and operation of that line of railroad, he was associated with the leading business men of Baltimore. He was for many years an elder of Baltimore meeting.

[8] The railroad this referred to by Elias Hicks was undoubtedly the section of the Baltimore and Ohio which ran from Baltimore to Ellicott's Mills, a distance of 15 miles. It was begun in 1828, and opened in Fifth month, 1830. Horses were at first used as motive power. This was the first railroad built in the United States.

Board of Directors. While not the first president of that company, he was elected president Sixth month 7, 1837, and served in that capacity until Fifth month 21, 1838.

Elias Hicks at points anticipated the present theory of suggestion touching bodily ailment, if he did not forestall some of the ideas regarding mental healing, and Christian Science. Writing to his son-in-law, Valentine Hicks, from Easton, Pa., Eighth month 15, 1819, he thus expressed himself:

"And indeed, in a strict sense, the mind or immortal spirit of man cannot be affected with disease or sickness, being endued with immortal powers; therefore all its apparent weakness lies in mere imagination, giving the mind a wrong bias and a wrong direction, but it loses more of its real strength, as to acting and doing. For instance, if at any time it admits those false surmises and imaginations, and by them is led to believe that its outward tabernacle is out of health and drawing towards a dissolution, and not being ready and willing to part with it, although little or nothing may be the disorder of the body, yet so powerfully strong is the mind under the influence of these wrong surmises that there seems at times to be no power in heaven or earth sufficient to arrest its progress, or stop its career, until it brings on actual disease, and death to the body, which, however, had its beginning principally in mere imagination and surmise. Hence we see the absolute necessity of thinking less about our mere bodily health, and much more about the mind, for if the mind is kept in a line of right direction, as it is that in which all its right health and strength consisteth, we need not fear any suffering to the body. For, if while the mind is under right direction, the body is permitted to fall under or into a state of affliction or disease, and the mind is kept in a state of due arrangement, it will prove a blessing and be sanctified to us as such, and in which we shall learn by certain experience that all things work together for good to those whose minds are preserved under the regulating influence of the love of God, which love casteth out all fear."

Elias Hicks was a firm opponent of the public school system, and especially the law which supported such schools by general taxation. His views regarding this latter are quite fully stated in a letter written Fifth 10th 24, 1820. It was written to Sylvanus Smith, and answered certain inquiries which had evidently been directed to Elias by this Friend. His objection to public schools, however, was partly based on what he considered moral and religious grounds. He said he had refrained from sending his children to any schools which were not under the immediate care of the Society of Friends. Observation, he said, lead him to believe that his "children would receive more harm than good by attending schools taught by persons of no religious principles, and among children whose parents were of different sects, and many very loose and unconcerned and vulgar in their lives and conduct." He also assumed that in the public schools his children would be demoralized "by the vicious conduct of many of the children, and sometimes even the teachers, which would be very degrading to their morals, and wounding to their tender minds." From his standpoint Friends could not consistently "take any part in those district schools, nor receive any part of the bounty given by the legislature of the state for their use."

Touching the question of parental authority and individual freedom, Elias Hicks also had opinions prejudicial to the public schools. In the letter under review he said:

"Believing the law that has established them to be arbitrary and inconsistent with the liberty of conscience guaranteed by the Constitution of the United States, and derogatory to right parental authority; as no doubt it is the right and duty of every parent to bring up and educate his children in that way he thinks is right, independent of the control of any authority under heaven (so long as he keeps them within the bounds of civil order). As the bringing up and right education of our children is a religious duty, and for which we are accountable to none but God only, therefore for the magistrate to interfere therewith by coercive means is an infringement upon the divine prerogative."

The observance of Thanksgiving Day, outside of New England, had not become a common thing in the time of Elias Hicks. Evidently about 1825, the Governor of New York issued a Thanksgiving Proclamation, which caused Elias to write an article. It was addressed to *The Christian Inquirer*,[9] and bore heavily against the whole thanksgiving scheme, especially when supported by the civil government. In his opinion wherever the magistrate recommended an observance of Thanksgiving Day, he was simply playing into the hands of the ecclesiastical power. We quote:

"Therefore the Governor's recommendation carries the same coercion and force in it, to every citizen, as the recommendation of the Episcopal Bishop would to the members of his own church. In this view we have the reason why the clergy men in our state call upon the civil magistrate to recommend one of their superstitious ceremonies. It is in order to coerce the citizens at large to a compliance with their dogmas, and little by little inure them to the yoke of ecclesiastical domination. I therefore conceive there is scarcely a subject that comes under our notice that lies more justly open to rebuke and ridicule than the thanksgiving days and fast days that are observed in our country, for there is nothing to be found in the writings of the New Testament to warrant such formality and superstition, and I fully believe in the way they are conducted they are altogether an abomination in the sight of the Lord, and tend more abundantly to bring a curse upon our nation than a blessing, as they too often end with many in festivity and drunkenness."

In closing his communication Elias says that in issuing his proclamation the Governor was simply "doing a piece of drudgery" for the clergy. The following, being the last paragraph in the communication referred to, sounds very

---

[9] The *Christian Inquirer* was a weekly newspaper in New York, started in 1824. It was of pronounced liberal tendencies. A good deal of its space was devoted to Friends, especially during the "separation" period.

much like the statements put forward by the extreme secularists in our own time:

"And has ne not by recommending a religious act united the civil and ecclesiastical authorities, and broken the line of partition between them, so wisely established by our enlightened Constitution, which in the most positive terms forbids any alliance between church and state, and is the only barrier for the support of our liberty and independence. For if that is broken down all is lost, and we become the vassals of priestcraft, and designing men, who are reaching after power by every subtle contrivance to domineer over the consciences of their fellow citizens."

It is not at all surprising that Elias Hicks was opposed to Free Masonry. On this subject he expressed himself vigorously. This opposition was based upon the secret character of the oath, and especially a solemn promise not to divulge the "secrets of Masonry, before he knows what the secrets are."

The anti-masonic movement, being the outcome of the mysterious disappearance of William Morgan from Batavia, New York, was at its height during the last years of Elias Hicks. It was claimed that Morgan was probably murdered because of a book published by him in 1826, exposing the secrets of Masonry. Some of the rumors connected with -this disappearance account for statements made by Elias Hicks in his criticism of the organization.

Touching the matter of exclusiveness on the part of Friends, Elias Hicks was a conservative of the conservatives. To keep aloof from things not connected with the Society he considered a virtue in itself. In referring to a meeting he attended in Goshen, Pa., he said:

"Had to caution Friends against mixing with the people in their human policies, and outward forms of government; showing that, in all ages, those who were called to be the Lord's people had been ruined, or suffered great loss, by such associations; and manifesting clearly by Scripture testimony, and other records, that our strength and preservation consisted in standing alone, and not to be counted among the people or nations, who were setting up party, and partial interest, one against another, which is the ground of war and bloodshed. These are actuated by the spirit of pride and wrath, which is always opposed to the true Christian spirit, which breathes 'peace on earth, and good will to all men.' Those, therefore, who are in the true Christian spirit cannot use any coercive force or compulsion by any means whatever; not being overcome with evil, but overcoming evil with good." [10]

In the article in which he condemned Masonry, Elias Hicks spoke vigorously in criticism of the camp meetings held by some of the churches. He called them "night revels," and considered them "a very great nuisance to civil society." He thought they were promoters of "licentiousness, in morality and drunkenness," and were more or less reproachful to the Christian name, "giving much occasion for infidels to scoff."

While at Elizabeth, in New Jersey, Elias wrote a letter [11] to a young man named Samuel Cox. It seems that this person contemplated studying for the ministry; that his grandmother was a Friend, and Elias labored with the grandson on her account. He said that "human study or human science" could not qualify a minister. In fact to suppose such a thing was to cast "the greatest possible indignity on the Divine Being, and on the gospel of our Lord Jesus Christ." Of course it was asserted that ministry came only by the power of the Spirit, and much Scripture was quoted to prove it. There is little in the writings of Elias Hicks to show that he considered that equipping the natural powers was helpful in making the spiritual inspiration effective.

It is evident, however, that Elias was not indifferent

---

[10] Journal, p. 76-77.

[11] Letter was dated, Fifth month 12, 1813.

Fac simile from page of a letter written by Elias Hicks to his wife, from Newtown, Pa., Tenth month 15, 1822. Near the middle of the sixth line the difference in writing evidently shows where the writer stopped and "sharpened" his quill pen. The name "Worton" in the last line should probably be Wharton.

to his own intellectual equipment. He was fond of quoting from books the things which fortified his own position. The following shows how he stored his mind with facts, from which he drew certain conclusions:

"Indisposition of body prevented my attending meeting. I therefore spent the day quietly at home, and in reading a portion of Mosheim's Ecclesiastical History of the Fifth Century, and which is indeed enough to astonish any sensible, considerate man, to think how the professors of that day could be hardy enough to call themselves Christians, while using every artifice that their human wisdom could invent to raise themselves to power and opulence, and endeavoring to crush down their opposers by almost every cruelty that power, envy and malice could inflict, to the entire scandal of the Christian name; and changing the pure, meek, merciful and undefiled religion of Jesus into an impure, unmerciful, cruel, bloody and persecuting religion. For each of those varied sects of professed Christians, in their turn, as they got the power of the civil magistrate on their side, would endeavor, by the sword, and severe edicts, followed by banishment, to reduce and destroy all those who dissented from them, although their opinions were not a whit more friendly to real, genuine Christianity than the tenets of their opposers; for all were, in great measure, if not entirely, adulterated and apostatized from the true spirit of Christianity, which breathes peace on earth, and good will to men." [12]

Elias Hicks believed that there was a sure way of determining conduct, whether it was from "one's own will," or whether it proceeded from the divine leading. In regard to this latter, he said:

"But the great error of the generality of professed Christians lies in not making a right distinction between the works that men do in their own will, and by the leadings of their own carnal wisdom, and those works that the true believer does, in the will and wisdom of God. For although the former, let them consist in what they will, whether in prayers, or preaching, or any other devotional exercises, are altogether evil; so on the contrary those of the latter, let them consist in what they may, whether in ploughing, in reaping, or in any handicraft labor, or in any other service, temporal or spiritual, as they will in all be accompanied with the peace and presence of their heavenly Father, so all they do will be righteous, and will be imputed to them as such."[13]

His contention regarding this matter is possibly more clearly stated in the following paragraph:

"The meeting was large, wherein I had to expose the danger of self-righteousness, or a trust in natural religion, or mere morality; showing that it was no more than the religion of Atheists, and was generally the product of pride and self-will; and, however good it may appear to the natural unregenerate man, is as offensive in the divine sight as those more open evils which appear so very reproachful to the eyes of men. I was favored by the spirit of truth, in a large, searching testimony, to the convicting and humbling many hearts, and comfort of the faithful."[14]

This is not unlike statements often made in modern revivals, touching the absolute uselessness of good works, without the operation of divine grace, in bringing salvation.

A broader view of goodness and its sources seems to have been taken by Clement, of Alexandria[15] who said: "For God is the cause of all good things; but of some primarily, as of the Old and New Testament; and of others by consequence, as philosophy. Perchance, too, philosophy was given to the Greeks directly and primarily, till the Lord should call the Greeks. For this was a schoolmaster to bring 'the Hellenic mind,' as the law, the Hebrews 'to Christ.' "[16]

---

[13] Journal, p. 218.

[14] Meeting at Uwchlan, Pa., Tenth month 22, 1798. Journal, p. 76.

[15] Titus Flavius Clemens, called sometimes St. Clement, and Clement of Alexandria in Church history, was born either at Athens or Alexandria about A. D. 153, and died about A. D. 220. He early embraced Christianity, and was among the most learned and philosophical of the Christian fathers.

[16] "Anti-Nicene Fathers," Vol. II. p. 305.

Some Points of Doctrine.

ELIAS HICKS had ideas of the future life, salvation, rewards and punishments, sometimes original, and in some
respects borrowed or adapted from prevalent opinions. But
in all conclusions reached he seems to have thought his own
way out, and was probably unconscious of having been a
borrower at all. He believed unfalteringly in the immortality of the soul, and held that the soul of man is immortal,
because it had its origin in an immortal God. Every sin
committed "is a transgression against his immutable and unchangeable law, and is an immortal sin, as it pollutes and
brings death on the immortal soul of man, which nothing
in heaven nor in the earth but God alone can extinguish
or forgive, and this he will never do, but upon his own
righteous and merciful conditions, which consist in nothing
more nor less than sincere repentance and amendment of
life."[1]

It will be noted that this statement was made near the
close of his career, and has been purposely selected because
it undoubtedly expressed his final judgment in the matter.
In all probability the words used were not meant to be
taken literally, such for instance as those referring to the
"death" of the soul. There is little, if any reason to think
that Elias Hicks believed in the annihilation of the sinner.

Touching sin he further explained his position. Whatever God creates is "immutably good." "Therefore if there

---

[1] From letter addressed to "A Friend," name not given, written
at Jericho, Second month 22, 1828.

is any such thing as sin and iniquity in the world, then God has neither willed it nor ordained it." [2] His position regarding this point caused him to antagonize and repudiate the doctrine of foreordination. From his standpoint this involved the creation of evil by the Almighty, a thoroughly preposterous supposition. Again, he held that if God had, "previous to man's creation, willed and determined all of his actions, then certainly every man stands in the same state of acceptance with him, and a universal salvation must take place: which I conceive the favorers of foreordination would be as unwilling as myself to believe." [3]

Three years after the declaration quoted above, Elias Hicks wrote a letter [4] to a person known as "J. N.," who was a believer in universal salvation. In this letter he revives his idea that foreordination and universal salvation are twin heresies, both equally mischievous. This letter is very long, containing nearly 4,000 words. The bulk of it deals with the theory of predestination, while some of it relates to the matter of sin and penalty. At one point the letter is censorious, nearly borders on the dogmatic, and is scarcely kind. We quote:

"Hadst thou, in thy researches after knowledge, been concerned to know the first step of wisdom—the right knowledge of thyself—such an humbling view of thy own insufficiency and entire ignorance of the Divine Being, and all his glorious attributes, would, I trust, have preserved thee from falling into thy present errors. Errors great indeed, and fatal in their consequences; for if men were capable of believing with confidence thy opinions, either as regards the doctrine of unconditional predestination and election, or the doctrine of universal salvation, both of which certainly and necessarily resolve in one, who could any longer call any thing he has his own? for all would

[2] Journal, p. 161.

[3] From funeral sermon delivered in 1814. Journal, p. 161.

[4] Letter dated Baltimore, Tenth month, 1817.

fall a prey to the villains and sturdy rogues of this belief.
And, indeed, a belief of these opinions would most assuredly
make thousands more of that description than there already
are; as every temptation to evil, to gratify the carnal desires, would be yielded to, as that which was ordained
to be; and of course would be considered as something
agreeable to God's good pleasure; and therefore not only
our goods and chattels would become a prey to every
ruffian of this belief, but even our wives and daughters
would fall victims to the superior force of the abandoned
and profligate, as believing they could do nothing but what
God had ordained to be. But we are thankful in the sentiment that no rational, intelligent being can possibly embrace, in full faith, these inconsistent doctrines; as they
are founded on nothing but supposition; and supposition
can never produce real belief, or a faith that any rational
creature can rely upon." [5]

We make no attempt to clear up the logical connection
between the doctrine of foreordination and the theory of
universal salvation, for it is by no means clear that the two
necessarily belong together. From the reasoning of Elias
Hicks it would seem that he considered salvation a transaction which made a fixed and final condition for the soul
at death, whereas the Universalist theory simply provides
for a future turning of all souls toward God. Surely the
supposition that the holding of the views of "J. N." would
bring the moral disorder and disaster outlined by his critic
had not then been borne out by the facts, and has not since.
Neither the believers in foreordination or universal salvation have been shown worse than other men, or more socially
dangerous.

"Sin," he says, "arises entirely out of the corrupt independent will of man; and which will is not of God's creating, but springs up and has its origin in man's disobedience
and transgression, by making a wrong use of his liberty." [6]

---

[5] "Letters of Elias Hicks," p. 28.

[6] "Letters of Elias Hicks," p. 30.

As the sin is of man's voluntary commission, the penalty is also to be charged to the sinner, and not to God. On this point Elias Hicks was clear in his reasoning and in his conclusions:

"Hence those who make their election to good, and choose to follow the teachings of the inward law of the spirit of God, are of course leavened into the true nature of God, and consequently into the happiness of God. For nothing but that which is of the nature of God can enjoy the happiness of God. But he who makes his election, or choice, to turn away from God's law and spirit, and govern himself or is governed by his own will and spirit, becomes a corrupt tree and although the same justice, wisdom, power, mercy and love are dispensed to this man as to the other, yet by his contrary nature, which has become fleshly, by following his fleshly inclinations, he brings forth corrupt fruit." [7]

Manifestly the idea that the Almighty punishes men for his own glory had no place in the thinking of the Jericho preacher.

The theory of sin and penalty held by Elias Hicks necessarily led him to hold opinions regarding rewards and punishments, and the place and manner of their application, at variance with commonly accepted notions. In fact, the apparent irregularity of his thinking in this particular was one of the causes of concern on his behalf on the part of his captious critics and some of his friends. One of the latter had evidently written him regarding this matter, and his reply is before us. [8] From it we quote:

"As to the subject relative to heaven and hell, I suppose what gave rise to that part of my communication (although I have now forgotten the particulars) was a concern that at that time as well as many other times has

---

[7] "Letters of Elias Hicks." p. 33.

[8] Letter dated Jericho, Third month 14, 1808.

sorrowfully impressed my mind, in observing the great ignorance and carnality that was not only prevailing among mankind at large, but more especially in finding it to be the case with many professing with us in relation to those things. An ignorance and carnality that, in my opinion, has been one great cause of the prevailing Atheism and Deism that now abounds among the children of men. For what reason or argument could a professed Christian bring forward to convince an Atheist or Deist that there is such a place as heaven as described and circumscribed in some certain limits and place in some distant and unknown region as is the carnal idea of too many professing Christianity, and even of many, I fear, of us? Or such a place as hell, or a gulf located in some interior part of this little terraqueous globe? But when the Christian brings forward to the Atheist or Deist reasons and arguments founded on indubitable certainty, things that he knows in his own experience every day through the powerful evidence of the divine law-giver in his own heart, he cannot fail of yielding his assent, for he feels as he goes on in unbelief and hardness of heart he is plunging himself every day deeper and deeper into that place of torment, and let him go whithersoever he will, his hell goes with him. He can no more be rid of it than he can be rid of himself. And although he flies to the rocks and mountains to fall on him, to deliver him from his tremendous condition, yet he finds all is in vain, for where God is, there hell is always to the sinner; according to that true saying of our dear Lord, 'this is the condemnation of the world that light is come into the world, but men love darkness rather than the light, because their deeds are evil.' Now God, or Christ (who are one in a spiritual sense), is this light that continually condemns the transgressor. Therefore, where God or Christ is, there is hell always to the sinner, and God, according to Scripture and the everyday experience of every rational creature, is everywhere present, for he fills all things, and by him all things consist. And as the sinner finds in himself and knows in his own experience that there is a hell, and one that he cannot possibly escape while he remains a sinner, so likewise the righteous know, and that by experience, that there is a heaven, but they know of none above the outward clouds and outward atmosphere. They have no experience of any such, but they know a heaven where God dwells, and know a sitting with him at seasons in heavenly places in Christ Jesus."

It will be remembered that Elias based salvation on repentance and amendment of life, but the bulk of his expression would seem to indicate that he held to the idea that repentance must come during this life. In fact, an early remark of his gives clear warrant for this conclusion.[9] He does not seem to have ever adopted the theory that continuity of life carried with it continuation of opportunity touching repentance and restoration of the soul.

From the twentieth century standpoint views like the foregoing would scarcely cause a ripple of protest in any well-informed religious circles. But eighty years ago the case was different. A material place for excessively material punishment of the soul, on account of moral sin and spiritual turpitude, was essential to orthodox standing in practically every branch of the Christian church, with possibly two or three exceptions. Elias Hicks practically admits that in the Society of Friends not a few persons held to the gross and materialistic conceptions which he criticised and repudiated.

The question of personal immortality was more than once submitted to him for consideration. After certain Friends began to pick flaws with his ideas and theories, he was charged with being a doubter regarding nearly all the common Christian affirmations, immortality included. There was little reason for misunderstanding or misrepresenting him in this particular, for, however he failed to make himself understood touching other points of doctrine, he was perfectly clear on this point. In a letter to Charles Stokes, of Rancocas, N. J., written Fourth month 3, 1829, he said:

"Can it be possibly necessary for me to add anything further, to manifest my full and entire belief of the immortality of the soul of man? Surely, what an ignorant creature

---

[9] See page 23 of this book.

must that man be that hath not come to the clear and full knowledge of that in himself. Does not every man feel a desire fixed in his very nature after happiness, that urges him on in a steady pursuit after something to satisfy this desire, and does he not find that all the riches and honor and glory of this world, together with every thing that is mortal, falls infinitely short of satisfying this desire? which proves it to be immortal; and can any thing, or being, that is not immortal in itself, receive the impress of an immortal desire upon it? Surely not. Therefore, this immortal desire of the soul of man never can be fully satisfied until it comes to be established in a state of immortality and eternal life, beyond the grave." [10]

There are not many direct references to immortality in the published sermons, although inferences in that direction are numerous. In a sermon at Darby, Pa., Twelfth month 7, 1826, he declared: "We see then that the great business of our lives is 'to lay up treasure in heaven.' " [11] In this case and others like it he evidently means treasure in the spiritual world. In his discourses he frequently referred to "our immortal souls" in a way to leave no doubt as to his belief in a continuity of life. His reference to the death of his young sons leave no room for doubt in the matter. [12]

In speaking of the death of his wife, both in his Journal and in his private correspondence, his references all point to the future life. "Her precious spirit," he said, "I trust and believe has landed safely on the angelic shore." Again, "being preserved together fifty-eight years in one unbroken bond of endeared affection, which seemed if possible to increase with time to the last moment of her life; and

---

[10] "Letters of Elias Hicks," p. 218.

[11] "The Quaker," Vol. IV, p. 127.

[12] See page 61 of this book.

which neither time nor distance can lessen or dissolve; but in the spiritual relation I trust it will endure forever." [13]

During the last ten years of the life of Elias Hicks he was simply overburdened answering questions and explaining his position touching a multitude of views charged against him by his critics and defamers. Among the matters thus brought to his attention was the miraculous conception of Jesus, and the various beliefs growing out of that doctrine. In an undated manuscript found among his papers and letters, and manifestly not belonging to a date earlier than 1826 or 1827, he pretty clearly states his theory touching this delicate subject. In this document he is more definite than he is in some of his published statements relating to the same matter. He asserts that there is a difference between "begetting and creating." He scouts as revolting the conception that the Almighty begat Jesus, as is the case in the animal function of procreation. On the other hand, he said: "But, as in the beginning of creation, he spake the word and it was done, so by his almighty power he spake the word and by it created the seed of man in the fleshly womb of Mary." In other words, the miraculous conception was a creation and not the act of begetting.

In his correspondence he repeatedly asserted that he had believed in the miraculous conception from his youth up. To Thomas Willis, who was one of his earliest accusers, he said that "although there appeared to me as much, or more, letter testimony in the account of the four Evangelists against as for the support of that miracle, yet it had not altered my belief therein." [14] It has to be admitted that the miraculous conception held by Elias Hicks was scarcely the doctrine of the creeds, or that held by evangelical Christians in the early part of the nineteenth

---

[13] Journal, p. 425.

[14] "Letters of Elias Hicks," p. 179.

century. His theory may be more rational than the popular conception and may be equally miraculous, but it was not the same proposition.

Whether Elias considered this a distinction without a difference we know not, but it is very certain that he did not consider the miracle or the dogma growing out of it a vital matter. He declared that a "belief therein was not an essential to salvation."[15] His reason for this opinion was that "whatever is essential to the salvation of the souls of men is dispensed by a common creator to every rational creature under heaven."[16] No hint of a miraculous conception, he held, had been revealed to the souls of men.

It is possible that in the minds of the ultra Orthodox, to deny the saving value of a belief in the miraculous conception, although admitting it as a fact, or recasting it as a theory, was a more reprehensible act of heresy than denying the dogma entirely. Manifestly Elias Hicks was altogether too original in his thinking to secure his own peace and comfort in the world of nineteenth-century theology.

When we consider the theory of the divinity of Christ, and the theory of the incarnation, we find Elias Hicks taking the affirmative side, but even here it is questionable if he was affirming the popular conception. Touching these matters he put himself definitely on record in 1827 in a letter written to an unnamed Friend. In this letter he says:

"As to the divinity of Christ, the son of the virgin— when he had arrived to a full state of sonship in the spiritual generation, he was wholly swallowed up into the divinity of his heavenly Father, and was one with his Father, with only this difference: his Father's divinity was underived, being self-existent, but the son's divinity was altogether derived from the Father; for otherwise he could not be the son of God, as in the moral relation, to be a son of man,

[15] "Letters of Elias Hicks," p. 178.

[16] "Letters of Elias Hicks," p. 178.

the son must be begotten by one father, and he must be in the same nature, spirit and likeness of his father, so as to say, I and my father are one in all those respects. But this was not the case with Jesus in the spiritual relation, until he had gone through the last institute of the law dispensation, viz., John's watery baptism, and had received additional power from on high, by the descending of the holy ghost upon him, as he came up out of the water. He then witnessed the fulness of the second birth, being now born into the nature, spirit and likeness of the heavenly Father, and God gave witness of it to John, saying, 'This is my beloved son, in whom I am well pleased.' And this agrees with Paul's testimony, where he assures us that as many as are led by the spirit of God, they are the sons of God." [17]

Just as he repudiated material localized places of reward and punishment, Elias Hicks disputed the presence in the world of a personal evil spirit, roaming around seeking whom he might ensnare and devour. In fact, in his theology there was no tinge of the Persian dualism. Satan, from his standpoint, had no existence outside man. He was simply a figure to illustrate the evil propensity in men. In the estimation of the ultra Orthodox to claim that there was no personal devil, who tempted our first parents in Eden, was second only in point of heresy to denying the existence of God himself—the two persons both being essential parts in the theological system to which they tenaciously held.

Touching this latter he thus expressed himself: "And as to what is called a devil or satan, it is something within us, that tempts us to go counter to the commands of God, and our duty to him and our fellow creatures; and the Scriptures tell us there are many of them, and that Jesus cast seven out of one woman." [18]

---

[17] "The Quaker," Vol. IV, p. 284.

[18] From letter to Charles Stokes, Fourth month 3, 1829. "Letters of Elias Hicks," p. 217.

He was charged with being a Deist, and an infidel of the Thomas Paine stripe, yet from his own standpoint there was no shadow of truth in any of these charges. His references to Atheism and Deism already cited in these pages afford evidence on this point. In 1798 he was at Gap in Pennsylvania, and in referring to his experience there he said:

"Whilst in this neighborhood my mind was brought into a state of deep exercise and travail, from a sense of the great turning away of many of us, from the law and the testimony, and the prevailing of a spirit of great infidelity and deism among the people, and darkness spreading over the minds of many as a thick veil. It was a time in which Thomas Paine's Age of Reason (falsely so called) was much attended to in those parts; and some, who were members in our Society, as I was informed, were captivated by his dark insinuating address, and were ready almost to make shipwreck of faith and a good conscience. Under a sense thereof my spirit was deeply humbled before the majesty of heaven, and in the anguish of my soul I said, 'spare thy people, O Lord, and give not thy heritage to reproach,' and suffer not thy truth to fall in the streets." [19]

Touching his supposed Unitarianism; there are no direct references to that theory in his published works. A letter written by Elias Hicks to William B. Irish, [20] Second month 11, 1821, is about the only reference to the matter. In this letter he says:

"In regard to the Unitarian doctrine, I am too much a stranger to their general tenets to give a decided sentiment, but according to the definition given of them by

[19] Journal, p. 70.

[20] William B. Irish lived in Pittsburg, and was a disciple of Elias Hicks, as he confessed to his spiritual profit. In a letter written to Elias from Philadelphia, Eleventh month 21, 1823, he said: "I tell you, you are the first man that ever put my mind in search of heavenly food." Whether he ever united with the Society we are not informed, although Elias expressed the hope that he might see his way clear to do so.

Dyche in his dictionary, I think it is more consistent and rational than the doctrine of the trinity, which I think fairly makes out three Gods. But as I have lately spent some time in perusing the ancient history of the church, in which I find that Trinitarians, Unitarians, Arians, Nestorians and a number of other sects that sprung up in the night of apostacy, as each got into power they cruelly persecuted each other, by which they evidenced that they had all apostatized from the primitive faith and practice, and the genuine spirit of Christianity, hence I conceive there is no safety in joining with any of those sects, as their leaders I believe are generally each looking to their own quarter for gain. Therefore our safety consists in standing alone (waiting at Jerusalem) that is in a quiet retired state, similar to the disciples formerly, until we receive power from on high, or until by the opening of that divine spirit (or comforter, a manifestation of which is given to every man and woman to profit withal) we are led into the knowledge of the truth agreeably to the doctrine of Jesus to his disciples."

In regard to the death and resurrection of Jesus, Elias Hicks considered himself logically and scripturally sound. although his ideas may not have squared with any prevalent theological doctrines. In reply to the query, "By what means did Jesus suffer?" he answered unhesitatingly, "By the hands of wicked men." A second query was to the effect, "Did God send him into the world purposely to suffer death?" Here is the answer:

"By no means; but to live a righteous and godly life (which was the design and end of God's creating man in the beginning), and thereby be a perfect example to such of mankind as should come to the knowledge of him and of his perfect life. For if it was the purpose and will of God that he should die by the hands of wicked men, then the Jews, by crucifying him, would have done God's will, and of course would all have stood justified in his sight, which could not be." . . . . . "But the shedding of his blood by the wicked scribes and Pharisees, and people of Israel, had a particular effect on the Jewish nation, as by this the topstone and worst of all their crimes, was filled up the measure of their iniquities, and which put an end to that dispensation, together with its law and covenant. That as

John's baptism summed up in one, all the previous water baptisms of that dispensation, and put an end to them, which he sealed with his blood, so this sacrifice of the body of Jesus Christ, summed up in one all the outward atoning sacrifices of the shadowy dispensation and put an end to them all, thereby abolishing the law having previously fulfilled all its righteousness, and, as saith the apostle, 'He blotted out the handwriting of ordinances, nailing them to his cross;' having put an end to the law that commanded them, with all its legal sins, and abolished all its legal penalties, so that all the Israelites that believed on him after he exclaimed on the cross 'It is finished,' might abstain from all the rituals of their law, such as circumcision, water baptisms, outward sacrifices, Seventh-day Sabbaths, and all their other holy days, etc." [21]

Continuing, he says: "Now all this life, power and will of man, must be slain and die on the cross spiritually, as Jesus died on the cross outwardly, and this is the true atonement, of which that outward atonement was a clear and full type." For the scriptural proof of his contention he quotes Romans VI, 3:4. He claimed that the baptism referred to by Paul was spiritual, and the newness of life to follow must also be spiritual.

The resurrection was also spiritualized, and given an internal, rather than an external, significance. Its intent was to awaken in "the believer a belief in the sufficiency of an invisible power, that was able to do any thing and every thing that is consistent with justice, mercy and truth, and that would conduce to the exaltation and good of his creature man."

"Therefore the resurrection of the dead body of Jesus that could not possibly of itself create in itself a power to loose the bonds of death, and which must consequently have been the work of an invisible power, points to and is a shadow of the resurrection of the soul that is dead in tres-

---

[21] All of the extracts above are from a letter to Dr. Nathan Shoemaker, of Philadelphia, written Third month 31, 1823. See "Foster's Report," pp. 422-23.

passes and sins, and that hath no capacity to quicken itself, but depends wholly on the renewed influence and quickening power of the spirit of God. For a soul dead in trespasses and sins can no more raise a desire of itself for a renewed quickening of the divine life in itself than a dead body can raise a desire of itself for a renewal of natural life; but both equally depend on the omnipotent presiding power of the spirit of God, as is clearly set forth by the prophet under the similitude of the resurrection of dry bones." Ezekiel, 37: 1.[22]

"Hence the resurrection of the outward fleshly body of Jesus and some few others under the law dispensation, as manifested to the external senses of man, gives full evidence as a shadow, pointing to the sufficiency of the divine invisible power of God to raise the soul from a state of spiritual death into newness of life and into the enjoyment of the spiritual substance of all the previous shadows of the law state. And by the arising of this Sun of Righteousness in the soul all shadows flee away and come to an end, and the soul presses forward, under its divine influence, into that that is within the veil, where our forerunner, even Jesus, has entered for us, showing us the way into the holiest of holies." [23]

We have endeavored to give such a view of the doctrinal points covered, as will give a fair idea of what Elias Hicks believed. Whether they were unsound opinions, such as should have disrupted the Society of Friends, and nearly shipwreck it on a sea of bitterness, we leave for the reader to decide. It should be stated, however, that the opinions herein set forth did not, by any means, constitute the subject matter of all, or possibly a considerable portion of the sermons he preached. There is room for the inquiry in our time whether a large amount of doctrinal opinion presented in our meetings for worship, even though it be of the kind in which the majority apparently believe, would not have a dividing and scattering effect.

---

[22] "The Quaker." Vol. IV, p. 286. Letter of Elias Hicks to an unknown friend.

[23] "The Quaker." Vol. IV, pp. 286-287. Letter of Elias Hicks to an unknown friend.

ELIAS HICKS

FROM PAINTING BY KETCHAM

CHAPTER XIV.

Before the Division.

No BIOGRAPHY of Elias Hicks could be even approximately adequate which ignored the division in the Society of Friends in 1827-1828, commonly, but erroneously, called "the separation." While his part in the trouble has been greatly exaggerated, inasmuch as he was made the storm-center of the controversy by his opponents, to consider the causes and influences which led to the difficulty, especially as they were either rightly or wrongly made to apply to Elias Hicks, is vital to a study of his life, and an appreciation of his labors.

We shall not be able to understand the matter at all, unless we can in a measure take ourselves back to the first quarter of the nineteenth century, and as far as possible appreciate the thought and life of that time. We must remember that a system of dogmatic theology, unqualified and untempered by any of the findings of modern scholarship, was the central and dominating influence in the religious world. Authority of some sort was the source of religious belief, and uniformity of doctrine the basis of religious fellowship.

The aftermath of the French Revolution appeared in a period of religious negation. Destructive, rather than constructive criticism was the ruling passion of the unchurched world. The conservative mind was burdened with apprehension, and the fear of a chaos of faith possessed the minds of the preachers, the theologians and the communicants of the so-called Orthodox Christian churches. The Unitarian uprising in New England had hopelessly divided the historic church of the Puritans, and the conservative Friends saw in every advance in thought the breaking up of what they considered the foundations of religion, and fear possessed them accordingly.

But more important than this is the fact that Friends had largely lost the historic perspective, touching their own origin. They had forgotten that their foundations were laid in a revolt against a prevalent theology, and the evil of external authority in religion. From being persecuted they had grown popular and prosperous. They therefore shrank from change in zion, and from the opposition and ostracism which always had been the fate of those who broke with approved and established religious standards. Without doubt they honored the heroism and respected the sacrifices of the fathers as the "first spreaders of truth." But they had neither the temper nor the taste to be alike heroic, in making Quakerism a progressive spirit, rather than a final refuge of a traditional religion.

An effort was made by the opponents of Elias Hicks to make it appear that what they were pleased to call his "unsoundness in doctrine," came late in life, and somewhat suddenly. But for this claim there is little if any valid evidence. His preaching probably underwent little vital change throughout his entire ministry. Turner, the English historian, says: "But the facts remain that until near the close of his long life Hicks was in general esteem, that there is no sign anywhere in his writings of a change of opinions, or new departure in his teaching."[1]

There is unpublished correspondence which confirms the opinion of Turner. This is true touching what might be called his theological as well as his sociological notions.

In a letter written to Elias Hicks in 1805, by James

---

[1] "The Quakers," Frederick Storrs Turner, p. 293.

Mott, Sr.,[2] reference is made to Elias having denied the
absolutely saving character of the Scriptures. In this connection the letter remarks: "I conceive it is no matter how
highly people value the Scriptures, provided they can only
be convinced that the spirit that gave them forth is superior
to them, and to be their rule and guide instead of them."

In 1806, in a sermon at Nine Partners, in Dutchess
County, New York, as reported by himself, he declared that
men can only by "faithful attention and adherence to the
aforesaid divine principle, the light within, come to know
and believe the certainty of those excellent Scripture doctrines, of the coming, life, righteous works, sufferings,
death and resurrection of Jesus Christ our blessed pattern:
and that *it is by obedience to this inward light only* that
we are prepared for admittance into the heavenly kingdom."[3]

It seems, however, that Stephen Grellet,[4] if we may
take the authority of his biographers, Hodgson[5] and
Guest,[6] as early as 1808, was fearful of the orthodoxy of
Elias Hicks, and probably based his fear on extracts like
the passage cited above. Whatever may be imagined to
the contrary, it is pretty certain that at no time for forty
years before his death did Elias Hicks preach doctrine that
would have been satisfactory to the orthodox theologians

[2] This James Mott was the father of Anne, who married Adam,
the father of James, the husband of Lucretia. James Mott, Sr. died
in 1823.

[3] Journal, p. 122.

[4] Stephen Grellet, born in Limoges, France, Eleventh month 2,
1773. A scion of the French nobility. Became interested in the Society
of Friends when about twenty years of age. Came to America in
1795, and was recorded a minister in Philadelphia, in 1798. Became
a New York business man in 1799. Made extensive religious visits in
various countries in Europe, and in many American states. Was also
active in philanthropic work. He died at Burlington, N. J., in 1855.
In his theology he was entirely evangelical.

[5] "Life of Stephen Grellet," Hodgson, p. 142.

[6] "Stephen Grellet," by William Guest, p. 73.

of his time, although he did not always antagonize the dogmas of the churches.

If Stephen Grellet ever had any personal interview with Elias Hicks regarding his "unsoundness," the latter was ignored by the latter. In Eighth month, 1808, some months after it is claimed the discovery was made by Grellet, the two men, with other Friends, were on a religious visit in parts of New England. In a letter to his wife, dated Danby, Vt., Eighth month 26, 1808, Elias says: "Stephen Grellet, Gideon Seaman, Esther Griffin and Ann Mott we left yesterday morning at a town called Middlebury, about eighteen miles short of this place, Stephen feeling a concern to appoint a meeting among the town's people of that place." Evidently no very great barrier existed between the two men at that time.

In any event no disposition seemed to exist to inaugurate a theological controversy in the Society of Friends, or to erect a standard of fellowship other than spiritual unity, until a decade after the claimed concern of Stephen Grellet. It appears that in 1818, Phebe Willis, wife of Thomas Willis, a recorded minister of Jericho Monthly Meeting, had a written communication with Elias, touching his doctrinal "soundness," Phebe being an elder. That the opposition began in Jericho, and that it was confined to the Willis family and one other in that meeting, seems to be a fairly well attested fact. In 1829, after the division in the Society had been accomplished, Elias Hicks wrote a letter to a friend giving a short history of the beginning of the trouble in Jericho, from which we take the following extract:

"The beginning of the rupture in our yearly meeting had its rise in our particular monthly meeting, and I have full evidence before me of both its rise and progress. The first shadow of complaint against me as to my doctrines was made by Thomas Willis, a member and minister of our own preparative meeting. He manifested his first uneasiness at the close of one of our own meetings nearly in these words, between him and myself alone. 'That he apprehended that I, in my public communication, lowered down the character of Jesus and the Scriptures of truth.' My reply to him was that I had placed them both upon the very foundation they each had placed themselves, and that I dare not place them any higher or lower. At the same time the whole monthly meeting, except he and his wife, as far as I knew, were in full unity with me, both as to my ministry and otherwise, but as they were both members of the meeting of ministers and elders they made the first public disclosure of their uneasiness. Thomas had an ancient mother, likewise a minister, that lived in the house with them; they so far overcame her better judgment as to induce her to take a part with them, although she was a very amiable and useful member, and one that I had always a great esteem for, and we had been nearly united together in gospel fellowship, both in public meetings and those for discipline, for forty years and upward."[7]

The meeting, through a judicious committee, tried to quiet the fears of Thomas Willis and wife, and bring them in unity with the vastly major portion of the meeting, but without success. These Friends being persistent in their opposition, they were suspended from the meeting of ministers and elders, but were permitted to retain their membership in the Society.

---

[7] Letter to Johnson Legg, dated Jericho, Twelfth month 15, 1829.

CHAPTER XV

First Trouble in Philadelphia.

TRANSFERRING the story of the opposition to the ministry of Elias Hicks to Philadelphia, it would appear that its first public manifestation occurred in 1819. During this year he made his fifth somewhat extended religious visit to the meetings within the bounds of Philadelphia Yearly Meeting. Elias was attending the monthly meeting then held in the Pine Street meeting-house, and obtained liberty to visit the women's meeting. While absent on this concern, the men's meeting did the unprecedented thing of adjourning, the breaking up of the meeting being accomplished by a few influential members. For a co-ordinate branch of a meeting for discipline to close while service was being performed in the allied branch in accord with regular procedure was considered irregular, if not unwarranted. The real inspiring cause for this conduct has been stated as follows by a contemporary writer:

"An influential member of this meeting who had abstained from the produce of slave labor came to the conclusion that this action was the result of his own will. He therefore became very sensitive and irritable touching references to the slavery question, and very bitter against the testimony of Elias Hicks. It is believed that this was one of the causes which led to the affront of Elias Hicks in the Pine Street Meeting aforesaid." [1]

It was claimed in the famous New Jersey chancery

[1] "A review of the general and particular causes which have produced the late disorders and divisions in the Yearly Meeting of Friends, held in Philadelphia," James Cockburn, 1829, p. 60.

case [2] by the Orthodox Friends, that there was precedent
for adjourning a meeting while a visiting minister in proper
order was performing service in a co-ordinate branch of the
Society. Be that as it may, the weight of evidence warrants
the conclusion that the incident at Pine Street was intended
as an affront to Elias Hicks. The conservative elements in
Philadelphia had evidently made up their minds that the
time had come to visit their displeasure upon the Long
Island preacher.

The incident referred to above must have occurred in
the latter part of Tenth month. Elias says in his Journal,
after mentioning his arrival in Philadelphia: "We were at
two of their monthly meetings and their quarterly meeting." [3] He makes no mention of the unpleasant occurrence.

There seems to have been no further appearance of
trouble in the latitude of Philadelphia until Eighth month,
1822. This time opposition appeared in what was evidently
an irregular gathering of part of the Meeting for Sufferings,
At this meeting Jonathan Evans is reported to have said:
"I understand that Elias Hicks is coming on here on his
way to Baltimore Yearly Meeting. Friends know that he
preaches doctrines contrary to the doctrines of our Society;
that he has given uneasiness to his friends at home, and
they can't stop him, and unless we can stop him here he
must go on." [4] This statement was only partially true, to
say the most possible for it. But a small minority of Elias'

---

[2] Foster's report, many times referred to in these pages, is a two-
volume work, containing the evidence and the exhibits in a case in
the New Jersey Court of Chancery. The examinations began Sixth
month 2, 1830, in Camden, N. J., before J. J. Foster, Master and Examiner in Chancery, and continued from time to time, closing Fourth
month 13, 1831. The case was brought to determine who should possess
the school fund, of the Friends' School, at Crosswick, N. J. The
decision awarded the fund to the Orthodox.

[3] Journal, p. 382.

[4] "Foster's Report," pp. 355-356.

home meeting were in any way "uneasy" about him, whatever may have been the character of his preaching. It stands to reason that had there been a general and united opposition to the ministry of Elias Hicks in his monthly meeting or in the New York Yearly Meeting at any time before the "separation," he could not have performed the service involved in his religious visits. It will also appear from the foregoing that the few opponents of Elias Hicks on Long Island had evidently planned to invoke every possible and conceivable influence, at the center of Quakerism in Philadelphia, to silence this popular and well-known preacher. At what point the influence so disposed became of general effect in the polity of the Society only incidentally belongs to the purpose of this book.

Out of the unofficial body [5] above mentioned, about a dozen in number, a small and "select" committee was appointed. The object was apparently to deal with Elias for remarks said to have been made by him at New York Yearly Meeting in Fifth month of that year, and reported by Joseph Whitall.

The minute under which Elias performed the visit referred to above was granted by his monthly meeting in Seventh month, and he promptly set out on his visit with David Seaman as his traveling companion. He spent nearly three months visiting meetings in New Jersey and in Bucks, Montgomery, Delaware and Chester Counties, Pennsylvania, reaching Baltimore the 25th of Tenth month, where he attended the Yearly Meeting. This appearance and service in Philadelphia, he states very briefly, and with no hint of the developing trouble, as follows:

"We arrived in Philadelphia in the early part of Twelfth month, and I immediately entered on the arduous concern

---

[5] "Foster's Report," 1831, Vol. I. See testimony of Joseph Whitall, p. 247. Also testimony of Abraham Lower, pp. 355-356.

which I had in prospect and which I was favored soon comfortably to accomplish. We visited the families composing Green Street Monthly Meeting, being in number one hundred and forty, and we also attended that monthly meeting and the monthly meeting for the Northern District. This closed my visit here, and set me at liberty to turn my face homeward."[6]

It will thus be seen that the charge of unsoundness was entered in Philadelphia Meeting for Sufferings soon after Elias started on his southern visit, but the latter was held practically in suspense for four months. In the meantime Elias was waited upon by a few elders, presumably in accordance with the action of the Meeting for Sufferings held in Eighth month. This opportunity was had when the visitor passed through Philadelphia en route to Baltimore. There is reason for believing that Elias succeeded in measureably satisfying this small committee. But there was evidently an element in Philadelphia that did not propose to be satisfied.

In Twelfth month, when Elias arrived in Philadelphia from his southern trip, and began his visits along the families of Green Street Monthly Meeting, a meeting of the elders of all the monthly meetings in the city was hastily called. A deputation from the elders sought an "opportunity" with Elias, and insisted that it be *private*.[7] His position was that he was not accountable to them for anything he had said while traveling with a minute as a minister. Elias finally consented, out of regard to some particular Friends, to meet the elders in Green Street meeting-house, provided witnesses other than the opposing elders could be present. Among those who accompanied Elias were John Comly, Robert Moore, John Moore and John Hunt.

[6] Journal, p. 394.

[7] "Foster's Report," pp. 359-360. "Cockburn's Review," p. 66.

When the meeting was held, however, the elders who opposed Elias said they could not proceed, their reason being that the gathering was not "select." In connection with this controversy letters passed between the opposing parties. One was signed by ten elders of Philadelphia, and is as follows:

"To ELIAS HICKS:
"Friends in Philadelphia having for a considerable time past heard of thy holding and promulgating doctrines different from and repugnant to those held by our religious society, it was cause of uneasiness and deep concern to them, as their sincere regard and engagement for the promotion of the cause of Truth made it very desirable that all the members of our religious society should move in true harmony under the leading and direction of our blessed Redeemer. Upon being informed of thy sentiments expressed by Joseph Whitall—that Jesus Christ was not the son of God until after the baptism of John and the descent of the Holy Ghost, and that he was no more than a man; that the same power that made Christ a Christian must make us Christians; and that the same power that saved Him must save us—many friends were affected therewith, and some time afterward, several Friends being together in the city on subjects relating to our religious society, they received an account from Ezra Comfort of some of thy expressions in the public general meeting immediately succeeding the Southern Quarterly Meeting lately held in the state of Delaware, which was also confirmed by his companion, Isaiah Bell, that Jesus Christ was the first man who introduced the gospel dispensation, the Jews being under the outward or ceremonial law or dispensation, it was necessary that there should be some outward miracle, as the healing of the outward infirmities of the flesh and raising the outward dead bodies in order to introduce the gospel dispensation; He had no more power given Him than man, for He was no more than man; He had nothing to do with the healing of the soul, for that belongs to God only; Elisha had the same power to raise the dead; that man being obedient to the spirit of God in him could arrive at as great, or a greater, degree of righteousness than Jesus Christ; that 'Jesus Christ thought it not robbery to be equal with God; neither do I think it robbery for man to be equal

with God'; then endeavored to show that by attending to that stone cut out of the mountain without hands, or the seed in man, it would make man equal with God, saying: for that stone in man was the entire God. On hearing which it appeared to Friends a subject of such great importance and of such deep welfare to the interest of our religious society as to require an extension of care, in order that if any incorrect statement had been made it should as soon as possible be rectified, or, if true, thou might be possessed of the painful concerns of Friends and their sense and judgment thereon. Two of the elders accordingly waited on thee on the evening of the day of thy arriving in the city, and although thou denied the statement, yet thy declining to meet these two elders in company with those who made it left the minds of Friends without relief. One of the elders who had called on thee repeated his visit on the next day but one, and again requested thee to see the two elders and the Friends who made the above statments which thou again declined. The elders from the different Monthly Meetings of the city were then convened and requested a private opportunity with thee, which thou also refused, yet the next day consented to meet them at a time and place of thy own fixing; but, when assembled, a mixed company being collected, the elders could not in this manner enter into business which they considered of a nature not to be investigated in any other way than in a select, private opportunity. They, therefore, considered that meeting a clear indication of thy continuing to decline to meet the elders as by them proposed. Under these circumstances, it appearing that thou art not willing to hear and disprove the charges brought against thee, we feel it a duty to declare that we cannot have religious unity with thy conduct nor with the doctrines thou art charged with promulgating.

"Signed, Twelfth month 19, 1822.

"CALEB PIERCE,
"LEONARD SNOWDEN,
"JOSEPH SCATTERGOOD,
"S. P. GRIFFITHS,
"T. STEWARDSON,
"EDWARD RANDOLPH,
"ISRAEL MAULE,
"ELLIS YARNALL,
"RICHARD HUMPHRIES,
"THOMAS WISTER."

To this epistle Elias Hicks made the following reply, two days having intervened:

"To CALEB PIERCE AND OTHER FRIENDS:

"Having been charged by you with unsoundness of principle and doctrine, founded on reports spread among the people in an unfriendly manner, and contrary to the order of our Discipline, by Joseph Whitall, as charged in the letter from you dated the 19th instant, and as these charges are not literally true, being founded on his own forced and improper construction of my words, I deny them, and I do not consider myself amenable to him, nor to any other, for crimes laid to my charge as being committed in the course of the sittings of our last Yearly Meeting, as not any of my fellow-members of that meeting discovered or noticed any such thing—which I presume to be the case, as not an individual has mentioned any such things to me, but contrary thereto. Many of our most valued Friends (who had heard some of those foul reports first promulgated by a citizen of our city) acknowledged the great satisfaction they had with my services and exercise in the course of that meeting, and were fully convinced that all those reports were false; and this view is fully confirmed by a certificate granted me by the Monthly and Quarterly Meetings of which I am a member, in which they expressed their full unity with me—and which meetings were held a considerable time after our Yearly Meeting, in the course of which Joseph Whitall has presumed to charge me with unsoundness of doctrine, contrary to the sense of the Monthly, Quarterly and Yearly Meetings of which I am a member, and to whom only do I hold myself amenable for all conduct transacted within their limits. The other charges made against me by Ezra Comfort, as expressed in your letter, are in general incorrect, as is proved by the annexed certificate; and, moreover, as Ezra Comfort has departed from gospel order in not mentioning his uneasiness to me when present with me, and when I could have appealed to Friends of that meeting to justify me; therefore, I consider Ezra Comfort to have acted disorderly and contrary to the discipline, and these are the reasons which induce me to refuse a compliance with your requisitions—considering them arbitrary and contrary to the established order of our Society.

"ELIAS HICKS.

"PHILADELPHIA, Twelfth month 21, 1822."

As already noted the charges in the letter of the ten elders were based on statements made by Joseph Whitall, supplemented by allegations by Ezra Comfort, as to what Elias had said in two sermons, neither of which was delivered within the bounds of Philadelphia Quarterly Meeting. The matters complained of are mostly subject to variable interpretation, and scarcely afford a basis for a religious quarrel, especially considering that the alleged statements were at the best garbled from quite lengthy discourses.

On the same day that Elias replied to the ten elders, three members of Southern Quarterly Meeting issued a signed statement regarding the charges of Ezra Comfort. It is as follows:

"We, the undersigned, being occasionally in the city of Philadelphia, when a letter was produced and handed us, signed by ten of its citizens, Elders of the Society of Friends, and directed to Elias Hicks, after perusing and deliberately considering the charges therein against him, for holding and propagating doctrines inconsistent with our religious testimonies, and more especially those said by Ezra Comfort and Isaiah Bell, to be held forth at a meeting immediately succeeding the late Southern Quarterly Meeting, and we being members of the Southern Quarter, and present at the said meeting, we are free to state, for the satisfaction of the first-mentioned Friends and all others whom it may concern, that we apprehend the charges exhibited by the two Friends named are without substantial foundation; and in order to give a clear view we think it best and proper here to transcribe the said charges exhibited and our own understanding of the several, viz., 'That Jesus Christ was the first man that introduced the Gospel Dispensation, the Jews being under the outward and ceremonial law or dispensation, it was necessary there should be some outward miracles, as healing the outward infirmities of the flesh and raising the outward dead bodies in order to introduce the gospel dispensation;' this in substance is correct. 'That he had no more power given him than man,' this sentence is incorrect; and also, 'That he had nothing to do with the healing of the soul, for that belongs to God only," is likewise incorrect; and the next sentence,

'That Elisha also had the same power to raise the dead' should be transposed thus to give Elias's expressions. 'By the same power it was that Elisha raised the dead.' 'That man being obedient to the spirit of God in him could arrive at as great or greater degree of righteousness than Jesus Christ,' this is incorrect; 'That Jesus Christ thought it not robbery to be equal with God,' with annexing the other part of the paragraph mentioned by the holy apostle would be correct. 'Neither do I think it robbery for man to be equal with God' is incorrect. 'Then endeavouring to show that by attending to that stone cut out of the mountain without hands or the seed in man it would make men equal with God' is incorrect; the sentence for that stone in man should stand thus: 'That this stone or seed in man had all the attributes of the divine nature that was in Christ and God.' This statement and a few necessary remarks we make without comment, save only that we were then of opinion and still are that the sentiments and doctrines held forth by our said friend, Elias Hicks, are agreeable to the opinions and doctrines held by George Fox and other worthy Friends of his time.

"ROBERT MOORE,
"THOMAS TURNER,
"JOSEPH G. ROWLAND. [8]

"12 10., 21, 1822."

First month 4, 1823, the ten elders sent a final communication to Elias Hicks, which we give in full:

"On the perusal of thy letter of the 21st of last month, it was not a little affecting to observe the same disposition still prevalent that avoided a select meeting with the elders, which meeting consistently with the station we are placed in and with the sense of duty impressive upon us, we were engaged to propose and urge to thee as a means wherein the cause of uneasiness might have been investigated, the Friends who exhibited the complaint fully examined, and the whole business placed in a clear point of view.

"On a subject of such importance the most explicit candour and ingenuousness, with a readiness to hear and give complete satisfaction ought ever to be maintained; this the Gospel teaches, and the nature of the case imperiously demanded it. As to the certificate which accompanied thy letter, made several weeks after the circumstances occurred, it is in several respects not only vague and ambiguous, but in others (though in different terms) it corroborates the statement at first made. When we take a view of the whole subject, the doctrines and sentiments which have been promulgated by thee, though under some caution while in this city, and the opinions which thou expressed in an interview between Ezra Comfort and thee, on the 19th ult., we are fully and sorrowfully confirmed in the conclusion that thou holds and art disseminating principles very different from those which are held and maintained by our religious society.

"As thou hast on thy part closed the door against the brotherly care and endeavours of the elders here for thy benefit, and for the clearing our religious profession, this matter appears of such serious magnitude, so interesting to the peace, harmony, and well-being of society, that we think it ought to claim the weighty attention of thy Friends at home." 9

One other communication closed the epistolary part of the controversy for the time being. It was a letter issued by twenty-two members of Southern Quarterly Meeting, concerning the ministerial service of Elias Hicks, during the meetings referred to in the charge of Ezra Comfort:

"We, the subscribers, being informed that certain reports have been circulated by Ezra Comfort and Isaiah Bell that Elias Hicks had propagated unsound doctrine, at our general meeting on the day succeeding our quarterly meeting in the 11th month last, and a certificate signed by Robert Moore, Joseph Turner and Joseph G. Rowland being read contradicting said reports, the subject has claimed our weighty and deliberate attention, and it is our united judgment that the doctrines preached by our said Friend on the day alluded to were the Truths of the Gospel, and that his labours of love amongst us at our particular meetings as

---

9 "Cockburn's Review," p. 76. As the signatures are the same as in the previous letter, repeating them seems unnecessary.

well as at our said quarterly meeting were united with by
all our members for aught that appears.

"And we believe that the certificate signed by the three
Friends above named is in substance a correct statement
of facts.

"ELISHA DAWSON,	GEORGE MESSECK,
"WILLIAM DOLBY,	WILLIAM W. MOORE,
"WALTER MIFFLIN,	JOHN COGWILL,
"DANIEL BOWERS,	SAMUEL PRICE,
"WILLIAM LEVICK,	ROBERT KEMP,
"ELIAS JANELL,	JOHN TURNER,
"JACOB PENNINGTON,	HARTFIELD WRIGHT,
"JONATHAN TWIBOND,	DAVID WILSON,
"HENRY SWIGGITT,	MICHAEL LOWBER,
"MICHAEL OFFLEY,	JACOB LIVENTON,
"JAMES BROWN,	JOHN COWGILL, JUNR.

"LITTLE CREEK, 2 10. 26th, 1823."

"I hereby certify that I was at the Southern Quarterly
Meeting in the 11th month last, but owing to indisposition
I did not attend the general meeting on the day succeeding,
and having been present at several meetings with Elias
Hicks, as well as at the Quarterly Meeting aforesaid, I can
testify my entire unity with the doctrines I have heard him
deliver.

"ANTHONY WHITELY." [10]

All of these communications, both pro and con, are
presented simply for what they are worth. When it comes
to determining what is or is not "unsound doctrine," we
are simply dealing with personal opinion, and not with
matters of absolute fact. This is especially true of a religious body that had never attempted to define or limit its
doctrines in a written creed.

The attempt of the Philadelphia elders to deal in a
disciplinary way with Elias Hicks on the score of the
manner or matter of his preaching was pronounced by his

[10] "Cockburn's Review," p. 78.

friends a usurpation of authority. It was held that the elders in question had no jurisdiction in the case, in proof of which the following paragraph in the Discipline of the Philadelphia Yearly Meeting was cited:

"And our advice to all our ministers is that they be frequent in reading the Scriptures of the Old and New Testaments; and if any in the course of their ministry shall misapply or draw unsound inferences or wrong conclusions from the text, or shall misbehave themselves in point of conduct or conversation, let them be admonished in love and tenderness by the elders or overseers where they live." [11]

It is undoubtedly true that a certain amount of encouragement came to the opponents of Elias Hicks in Philadelphia from some Friends on Long Island, and from three or four residents of Jericho, but they did not at that time at least officially represent any meeting of Friends at Jericho, either real or pretended. Thus far in the controversy the aggressors were confined to those who at that time were considered the "weight of the meeting," and who at best represented only the so-called "select" meeting, and not the Society at large. At the beginning at least the trouble was an affair of the ministers and elders. It later affected the whole Society, by the efforts of the leaders on both sides.

Incidents are not wanting to show that up to the very end of the controversy the rank and file of Friends had little vital interest in the matters involved in the trouble. It is related on good authority that two prominent members of Nine Partners Quarterly Meeting in Dutchess County, New York, husband and wife, made a compact before attending the meeting in Eighth month, 1828, feeling that the issue would reach its climax at that time. They agreed that whichever side retained control of the organization and the meeting-house would be considered by them the meeting, and receive their support. We mention this as undoubtedly representing the feeling in more than one case. The fact that it took practically a decade of excitement and manipulation, to create the antagonisms, personal and otherwise, which resulted in an open rupture, shows how little disposed the majority of Friends were to disrupt the Society.

CHAPTER XVI.

The Time of Unsettlement.

BETWEEN the trouble related in the last chapter and the culmination of the disturbance in the Society of Friends, in 1827-1828, there was an interval of four or five years. This period was by no means one of quiet. On the other hand it was one of confusion, in the midst of which the forces were at work, and the plans perfected which led up logically to the end.

It will be remembered that the last communication of the Philadelphia elders sent to Elias Hicks was dated First month 4, 1823. They had manifestly failed to silence the preacher from Jericho, or to greatly alarm him with their charges of heresy. Just eleven days after the epistle in question was written, the Meeting for Sufferings of Philadelphia Yearly Meeting assembled. This meeting issued a singular document,[1] said by the friends of Elias Hicks to have been intended as a sort of "Quaker Creed," but this was vigorously denied by those responsible for its existence. The statement of doctrine, which was as follows, was duly signed by Jonathan Evans, clerk, "on behalf of the meeting:"

"At a Meeting for Sufferings held in Philadelphia the 17th of the First month, 1823, an essay containing a few brief extracts from the writings of our primitive Friends on several of the doctrines of the Christian religion, which have been always held, and are most surely believed by us,

---

[1] The title of the production was as follows: Extracts from the Writings of Primitive Friends, concerning the Divinity of Our Lord and Saviour, Jesus Christ. Published by the direction of the Meeting for Sufferings, held in Philadelphia. Solomon W. Conrad, printer.

being produced and read; on solid consideration they appeared so likely to be productive of benefit, if a publication thereof was made and spread among our members generally, that the committee appointed on the printing and distribution of religious books are directed to have a sufficient number of them struck off and distributed accordingly, being as follows:

"We have always believed that the Holy Scriptures were written by divine inspiration, that they are able to make wise unto salvation through faith which is in Christ Jesus, for, as holy men of God spake as they were moved by the Holy Ghost, they are therefore profitable for doctrine, for reproof, for correction, for instruction in righteousness, that the man of God may be perfect, thoroughly furnished unto all good works. But they are not or cannot be subjected to the fallen, corrupt reason of man. We have always asserted our willingness that all our doctrines be tried by them, and admit it as a positive maxim that whatsoever any do (pretending to the Spirit) which is contrary to the Scriptures be accounted and judged a delusion of the devil.

"We receive and believe in the testimony of the Scriptures simply as it stands in the text. 'There are three that bear record in heaven, the Father, the Word, and the Holy Ghost, and these three are one.'

"We believe in the only wise, omnipotent and everlasting God, the creator of all things in heaven and earth, and the preserver of all that he hath made, who is God over all blessed forever.

"The infinite and most wise God, who is the foundation, root and spring of all operation, hath wrought all things by his eternal Word and Son. This is that Word that was in the beginning with God and was God, by whom all things were made, and without whom was not anything made that was made. Jesus Christ is the beloved and only begotten Son of God, who, in the fulness of time, through the Holy Ghost, was conceived and born of the Virgin Mary; in him we have redemption through his blood, even the forgiveness of sins. We believe that he was made a sacrifice for sin, who knew no sin; that he was crucified for us in the flesh, was buried and rose again the third day by the power of his Father for our justification, ascended up into heaven and now sitteth at the right hand of God.

"As then that infinite and incomprehensible Fountain

of life and motion operateth in the creatures by his own eternal word and power, so no creature has access again unto him but in and by the Son according to his own blessed declaration, 'No man knoweth the Father but the Son, and he to whom the Son will reveal him.' Again, 'I am the way, the truth, and the life; no man cometh unto the Father but by me.' Hence he is the only Mediator between God and man for having been with God from all eternity, being himself God, and also in time partaking of the nature of man; through him is the goodness and love of God conveyed to mankind, and by him again man receiveth and partaketh of these mercies.

"We acknowledge that of ourselves we are not able to do anything that is good, neither can we procure remission of sins or justification by any act of our own, but acknowledge all to be of and from his love, which is the original and fundamental cause of our acceptance. 'For God so loved the world that he gave his only begotten Son that whosoever believeth in him should not perish, but have everlasting life.'

"We firmly believe it was necessary that Christ should come, that by his death and sufferings he might offer up himself a sacrifice to God for our sins, who his own self bear our sins in his own body on the tree; so we believe that the remission of sins which any partake of is only in and by virtue of that most satisfactory sacrifice and no otherwise. For it is by the obedience of that one that the free gift is come upon all to justification. Thus Christ by his death and sufferings hath reconciled us to God even while we are enemies; that is, he offers reconciliation to us, and we are thereby put into a capacity of being reconciled. God is willing to be reconciled unto us and ready to remit the sins that are past if we repent.

"Jesus Christ is the intercessor and advocate with the Father in heaven, appearing in the presence of God for us, being touched with a feeling of our infirmities, sufferings, and sorrows; and also by his spirit in our hearts he maketh intercession according to the will of God, crying abba, Father. He tasted death for every man, shed his blood for all men, and is the propitiation for our sins; and not for ours only, but also for the sins of the whole world. He alone is our Redeemer and Saviour, the captain of our salvation, the promised seed, who bruises the serpent's head; the alpha and omega, the first and the last. He is our wisdom, righteousness, justification and redemption;

neither is there salvation in any other, for there is no other name under heaven given among men whereby we may be saved.

"As he ascended far above all heavens that he might fill all things, his fulness cannot be comprehended or contained in any finite creature, but in some measure known and experienced in us, as we are prepared to receive the same, as of his fulness we have received grace for grace. He is both the word of faith and a quickening spirit in us, whereby he is the immediate cause, author, object and strength of our living faith in his name and power, and of the work of our salvation from sin and bondage of corruption.

"The Son of God cannot be divided from the least or lowest appearance of his own divine light or life in us, no more than the sun from its own light; nor is the sufficiency of his light within set up or mentioned in opposition to him, or to his fulness considered as in himself or without us; nor can any measure or degree of light received from Christ be properly called the fulness of Christ; or Christ as in fulness, nor exclude him from being our complete Saviour. And where the least degree or measure of this light and life of Christ within is sincerely waited in, followed and obeyed there is a blessed increase of light and grace known and felt; as the path of the just it shines more and more until the perfect day, and thereby a growing in grace and in the knowledge of God and of our Lord and Saviour Jesus Christ hath been and is truly experienced.

"Wherefore we say that whatever Christ then did, both living and dying, was of great benefit to the salvation of all that have believed and now do and that hereafter shall believe in him unto justification and acceptance with God; but the way to come to that faith is to receive and obey the manifestation of his divine light and grace in the conscience, which leads men to believe and value and not to disown or undervalue Christ as the common sacrifice and mediator. For we do affirm that to follow this holy light in the conscience and to turn our minds and bring all our deeds and thoughts to it is the readiest, nay, the only right way, to have true, living and sanctifying faith in Christ as he appeared in the flesh; and to discern the Lord's body, coming and sufferings aright, and to receive any real benefit by him as our only sacrifice and mediator, according to the beloved disciple's emphatical testimony, 'If we walk in the light as he (God) is in the light we have fellowship one with another, and the blood of Jesus Christ his son cleanseth us from all sin.'

"By the propitiatory sacrifice of Christ without us we, truly repenting and believing, as through the mercy of God, justified from the imputation of sins and transgressions that are past, as though they had never been committed; and by the mighty work of Christ within us the power, nature and habits of sin are destroyed; that as sin once reigned unto death even so now grace reigneth through righteousness unto eternal life by Jesus Christ our Lord." [2]

This deliverance is almost as theological and dogmatic as the Westminster Confession. It scarcely contains a reference to the fundamental doctrine of George Fox. It is not too much to say that if it was the belief of the "primitive" Friends, there was little reason, touching points of doctrine, for the preaching of Fox, or the first gathering of the Society. All the ground covered by this doctrinal statement was amply treated in the Articles of Religion of the Church of England, and the Confession of the Presbyterians.

The above document was issued without quotation marks, or any indication as to what "primitive" Friends were responsible for the sentiments contained in its various parts. By careful examination it will be seen that one sentence, at least, is from Barclay's Apology, "but it proves to be a garbled quotation." We refer to the following sentence in the second paragraph in the above article, relating to the Scriptures: "But they are not or cannot be subjected to the fallen, corrupt reason of man." Barclay's complete statement is here given:

"Yet, as the proposition itself concludeth, to the last part of which I now come, it will not from thence follow that these divine revelations are to be subjected to the examination either of the outward testimony of Scripture or of the human or natural reason of man, as to a more

---

[2] "The Friend, or Advocate of Truth," Vol. I, pp. 152-154.

noble and certain rule or touchstone; for the divine revelation and inward illumination is that which is evident by itself, forcing the well-disposed understanding and irresistibly moving it to assent by its own evidence and clearness, even as the common principles of natural truths to bend the mind to a natural assent."[3]

It will be seen clearly that the reference in the document issued by the Meeting for Sufferings was not only a misquotation from Barclay, but also misrepresented his meaning. The latter is particularly true if we refer to the top of the same page that contains the above extract, where he says: "So would I not have any reject or doubt the certainty of that unerring Spirit which God hath given his children as that which can alone guide them into all truth, because some have falsely pretended to it."[4] It will thus appear clear that Elias Hicks, and not the Meeting for Sufferings, was supported by Barclay.

The reference in the third paragraph in the foregoing "declaration" to the "three that bear record in heaven" is a quotation from 1 John 5:7. It is entirely omitted from the Revised Version, and thorough scholars in the early years of the nineteenth century were convinced that the passage was an interpolation.

The statement of belief prepared by the Meeting for Sufferings was not approved by the Yearly Meeting, so nothing was really accomplished by the compilation, if such it was.

Considering the order of the events recorded, it is hard not to conceive that the attempt to promulgate a "declaration of faith" by the Yearly Meeting was really intended for personal application to Elias Hicks. Had the plan succeeded, the elders could easily have attempted to silence the

---

[3] "Barclay's Apology." Edition of Friends' Book Store, 304 Arch Street, Philadelphia, 1877, p. 68.

[4] "Barclay's Apology." Edition of 1877, p. 68.

Daniel Mudg's Land

No. 7   A rods   4·97
N88½W

No. 6   A 4, 117 rods
S88W

No. 5   5 Acres
S81½W

No. 4   5 Acres
S81½W

No. 3   5 Acres
S81½W

No. 2   5 Acres
S81½W

No. 1   A. 66 rods.

No. 11   A r 6·96
S88W

No. 10   A   5·
S88W

No. 9   5 Acres
S88W

Lot No. 8   5 Acres
S88 W 49

Richard Townsends Land

Onderdonk's Land

Hendrick Ondordonk's Land

At the request of Thomas Pearsall
I have surveyed and devided the
land contained in the annexed plan
it being a certain piece of Wood
land situate on the north side of
the harbour hill. each lot contains in quantity as therein
exprest, laid down by a scale of
20 rods to the inch and performed
the 5th day of the 6th Mo. 1804
By ——— Elias Hicks

To Harry Head Harbour
by Jeremiah Robbins

Highway 32 Wide

No. 1 = 4, 66 Square.
2 = 5 Acres
3 = 5 Ditto
4 = 5 Ditto
5 = 5 Ditto
6 = 4: 117 Square Rods
7 = 4: 97 Square Rods
8 = 5 Ditto
9 = 5 Ditto
10 = 5 Ditto
is placed at each
of every lot a good Locust Stake
11 = 6: 96

S
E   W
N

Jericho preacher in Philadelphia, on the ground that he was "unsound" touching the doctrine promulgated by the Yearly Meeting.

The task of detailing all of the doings of this period would be too difficult and distasteful to be fully recorded in this book. That the unfriendly conduct was by no means all on one side is painfully true. Still, as the determination of the Philadelphia elders to deal with Elias Hicks, and stop his ministry if possible, was continued, the effort cannot be ignored.

In First month, 1825, the elders presented a charge of unsoundness against Elias Hicks in the Preparative Meeting of Ministers and Elders, the intent being to have the charge forwarded to the monthly meeting, but this action was not taken. With phenomenal persistence one of the elders introduced the subject in the monthly meeting, and secured the appointment of a committee to investigate the merits of the case. This committee made a report unfavorable to Elias Hicks, which report, his friends claimed was improperly entered on the minutes. A vigorous, but by no means a united effort was made to get this report forwarded to Jericho Monthly Meeting, but this failed. One of the incidents of this attempt against Elias Hicks was the disownment of a member of the Northern District Monthly Meeting, for remarks made in Western District Monthly Meeting. The report of the committee against Elias was under consideration, when the visitor arose and said : "If it be understood by the report—if it set forth and declare, that Elias Hicks, the last time he was in this house, preached doctrines contrary to the Holy Scriptures, or contrary to our first or primitive Friends, being present at that time, I stand here as a witness that it is utterly false." [5] Although this Friend was disowned by his monthly meet-

---

ing he was reinstated by the Quarterly Meeting. It should
be said that the report of unsoundness referred to, contained this specific charge: "We apprehend that Elias
Hicks expressed sentiments inconsistent with the Holy
Scriptures, and the religious principles our Society has held
from its first rise."

The trouble in Philadelphia was renewed in an aggravated form in First month, 1827 when Elias Hicks appeared in the city on another religious visit. Of course
the atmosphere had been charged with all sorts of attacks
regarding the venerable preacher. Under such conditions
no special advertising was necessary to get a crowd. The
populace was curious, not a few wanted to hear and see,
for themselves, this man about whom so many charges had
been made. As a matter of course the meeting-houses
were crowded beyond their capacity. It was alleged by
Orthodox Friends that the meetings were disorderly, which
may have been literally true. But the tumult was increased
by injecting an element of controversy, into the First-day
afternoon meeting in Western meeting-house, on the part
of an Orthodox elder. All the evidence goes to show that
Elias attempted to quiet the tumult. He seems to have been
willing to accord liberty of expression to his opponents.
The matter was taken into Western Monthly Meeting, a
committee entering the following charge: "That a large
and disorderly concourse of people were brought together,
at an unseasonable hour, and under circumstances that
strongly indicated a design to preoccupy the house to the
exclusion of most of the members of our meeting, and to
suppress in a riotous manner any attempt that might be
made to maintain the doctrine and principles of our religious
society, in opposition to the views of Elias Hicks." [6]

---

6 "Cockburn's Review," p. 100.

The literal truthfulness of this charge in every particular may be at least mildly questioned. It must be remembered that of the Friends in Philadelphia at that time, the Orthodox were a minority of about one to three. The majority of Friends felt that much of the trouble was personal, and they undoubtedly flocked to hear the traduced preacher. The outside crowd that came could not rightfully or wisely have been kept from attending public meetings. Both parties had been sowing to the wind, and neither could validly object to the whirlwind that inevitably came. Still Western Monthly Meeting proposed to deal with a visiting minister from another yearly meeting, on points of doctrine, and there can be little doubt that arbitrary proceedings of this sort had quite as much, if not more, to do with kindling the fires of "separation," as the preaching of Elias Hicks.

. Rapidly the trouble ran back to the opposition raised by the elders in 1822. Eventually Green Street Monthly Meeting became the center of Society difficulty. It will be remembered that in the year last written that monthly meeting had enjoyed a family visitation from Elias Hicks, and had subsequently given him a minute of approval. After this one of the elders, who acquiesced in this action, joined the other nine in written disapproval of Elias Hicks. The major portion of the monthly meeting proposed to take the inconsistent conduct of this elder under care, and the latter was handed over to the overseers. In thus hastily invoking the discipline, Green Street Monthly Meeting made an apparent error of judgment, even admitting that the spirit of the transaction was not censurable. This brought the Quarterly Meeting of Ministers and Elders precipitously into the case. Finally Green Street Monthly Meeting released the Friend in question from his station as elder. A question arose on which there was a sharp discussion as to whether elders were independent of the overseers in the exercise of their official duties. A long line of conduct followed, finally resulting in the Quarterly Meeting of Ministers and Elders sending a report to the general quarterly meeting, amounting to a remonstrance against Green Street Monthly Meeting. This appeared to be a violation of Discipline, which said: "None of the said meetings of ministers and elders are in anywise to interfere with the business of any meeting for discipline."[7] These matters, with the remonstrance of the released Green Street elder, would therefore seem to have been irregularly brought before the quarterly meeting. It was claimed by the friends of Elias Hicks that he had broken no rule of discipline; that the charge, that he held "sentiments inconsistent with the Scriptures, and the principles of Friends," was vague as to its matter, and purely personal as to the manner of its circulation. Up to this point it should be remembered, the controversy was almost entirely centered on Elias Hicks.

This matter dragged along, a source of constant disturbance, appearing in perhaps a new form in the Quarterly Meeting of Ministers and Elders in Eighth month, 1826. The immediate action involved appointing a committee to assist the Preparative Meeting of Ministers and Elders of Green Street Monthly Meeting, the assumed necessity in the case being the reported unsoundness of a Green Street minister, a charge to this effect having been preferred by one member only. The situation, however, caused an abatement in answering the query relating to love and unity. While these transactions were going on along the ministers and elders, Green Street Monthly Meeting took action which removed two of its elders from that station in the Society. The two deposed elders took their grievances to the general

---

[7] Rules of Discipline of the Yearly Meeting of Friends, held in Philadelphia, 1806, p. 67.

quarterly meeting. While the quarterly meeting would not listen to a statement of grievances, yet a committee to go over the whole case was appointed. The committee thus appointed, without waiting any action by the quarterly meeting, transformed the removal of the aggrieved elders into an appeal, and then demanded that Green Street Monthly Meeting turn over to that committee all the minutes relating to the case of the two elders. This the Green Street Meeting refused to do. Although the case had never been before the quarterly meeting, the committee of inquiry reported to the full meeting, that all of the action of Green Street Monthly Meeting relating to the two elders should be annulled. It was claimed that, by virtue of the leadership which the Orthodox had in the quarterly meeting, a precedent had been established which gave committees the right to exceed the power conferred upon them by the meeting which appointed them. The committee had not been appointed to decide a case, but to investigate a complaint.

Following this experience, after much wrangling, and in the midst of manifest disunity, and against what it was claimed was the manifest opposition of the major portion of the meeting, the quarterly meeting in Eleventh month, 1826, appointed a committee to visit the monthly meetings. This committee was manifestly one-sided, but could have no possible disciplinary service from extending brotherly care. Nevertheless at the quarterly meeting in Fifth month, 1827, this committee, for presumed gospel labor, reported that the large Green Street Monthly Meeting should be laid down, and its members attached to the Northern District Monthly Meeting. It is not necessary to enter into any argument as to the right of a quarterly meeting, under our system, to lay down an active monthly meeting, without that meeting's consent. The laying down of Green Street Monthly Meeting followed the "separation" in the yearly meeting. It should be said that in Second month, 1827, Green Street

Monthly Meeting, attempted to secure consent from the quarterly meeting to transfer itself to Abington Quarterly Meeting, and subsequently this was done.

The claim was made, and with some show of reason, that the various lines of conduct taken against Green Street Monthly Meeting, were incited by a desire to punish this meeting for its friendly interest in Elias Hicks.

We are rapidly approaching the point where the Society troubles in Philadelphia ceased to directly relate to Elias Hicks. It will be remembered that there was trouble touching the preaching of Elias coming by way of Southern Quarterly Meeting in 1822. The facts indicate that a majority of that meeting was quite content to let matters rest. It seems, however, that two members of the Meeting for Sufferings from that quarter had misrepresented their constituency in the Hicks controversy. Therefore in 1826 that quarterly meeting discontinued the service of the two members of the Meeting for Sufferings, supplying their places with new appointments. This action was objected to by the full meeting, the majority holding that members could not have their service discontinued by the constituent bodies which appointed them. An attempt was made to convince Southern Quarterly Meeting that it was improper and illegal to appoint new representatives, if the old ones were willing to serve. It was also claimed that it was "never intended to release the representatives from a quarterly meeting to the Meeting for Sufferings, except at their own request." [8] Surely the Discipline then operative gave no warrant for such an inference. [9] Assuming that the above contention was valid, the Meeting for Sufferings

---

[8] "Cockburn's Review," p. 170.

[9] Rules of Discipline of the Yearly Meeting of Friends, held in Philadelphia, 1806, p. 54-55.

would simply have become a small hierarchy in the Society, never to be dissolved, except at its own request.

It would seem, however, that the rules governing the Meeting for Sufferings were especially made to guard against just such an exercise of power as has been mentioned. The Discipline under the heading, "Meeting for Sufferings," contained this provision: "The said meeting is not to meddle with any matter of faith or discipline, which has not been determined by the yearly meeting." [10] This will make it plain why there was such an anxiety that the statement of doctrine issued in 1823,[11] should be endorsed by the yearly meeting, and when that failed, how utterly the statement was without authority or binding force on the Society in general or its members in particular.

[10] The same, p. 55.

[11] See page 139 of this book.

CHAPTER XVII.

Three Sermons Reviewed.

WE HAVE reached the point where it would seem in order to consider the matter contained in some of the sermons preached by Elias Hicks, in order to determine, if we can, what there was about the matter or the manner of his ministry, which contributed to the controversy, personal and theological, which for several years disturbed the Society of Friends.

The trouble was initiated, and for some time agitated, by comparatively few people. Two or three Friends began talking about what Elias said, from memory. Later they took long-hand notes of his sermons, in either case using isolated and disconnected sentences and expressions. Taken from their association with the balance of the sermon, and passed from mouth to mouth by critics, they assumed an exaggerated importance, and stood out boldly as centers of controversy.

All of the evidence goes to show that little attempt was made to give printed publicity to these discourses, until the preacher had been made famous by the warmth and extent of the controversy over the character of his preaching.

A volume of twelve sermons preached by Elias Hicks at various points in Pennsylvania in 1824 was published the following year in Philadelphia by Joseph and Edward Parker. These discourses were taken in short-hand by Marcus T. C. Gould. Two years later, in 1827, Gould began the publication of "The Quaker," which contained sermons by Elias, and a few other ministers in the Society. In his advertisement of the first volume of this publication, after stating the fact of the controversy which was rapidly dividing the Society of Friends in two contending parties. Gould says:

"At this important crisis, the reporter and proprietor of the following work was employed by the joint consent of both parties, to record in meeting the speeches of the individual whose doctrines were by some pronounced sound, and by others unsound. Since that period he has continued to record the language of the same speaker, and others who stand high as ministers in the Society, and the members have continued to read his reports, as the only way of arriving at the truth, in relation to discourses which were variously represented."

It is not our purpose in this chapter to give sermons or parts of sermons in detail. On the other hand, to simply review a few of these discourses as samples, because at the time of their delivery they called out opposition from Orthodox Friends. It may be fairly inferred that they contained in whole or in part the points of doctrinal offending in the estimation of the critics of Elias Hicks.

The first of the series of sermons especially under review, was delivered in the Pine Street meeting house, Philadelphia, Twelfth month 10, 1826. At the conclusion of this sermon Jonathan Evans arose, and spoke substantially as follows:

"I believe it to be right for me to say, that our Society has always believed in the atonement, mediation, and intercession of our Lord and Saviour Jesus Christ—that by him all things were created, in heaven and in earth, both visible and invisible, whether they be thrones, principalities, or powers.

"We believe that all things were created by him, and for him; and that he was before all things, and that by him all things consist. And any doctrine which goes to invalidate these fundamental doctrines of the Christian religion we cannot admit, nor do we hold ourselves accountable for.

"Great efforts are making to make the people believe that Jesus Christ was no more than a man, but we do not

20

believe any such thing, nor can we receive any such doctrine, or anything which goes to inculcate such an idea.

"We believe him to be King of kings, and Lord of lords, before whose judgment seat every soul shall be arraigned and judged by him. We do not conceive him to be a mere man; and we therefore desire, that people may not suppose that we hold any such doctrines, or that we have any unity with them."

Isaac Lloyd said: "I unite with Jonathan Evans—we never have believed that our blessed Lord and Saviour, Jesus Christ, came to the Jews only; for he was given for God's salvation, to the ends of the earth." [1]

To these doctrinal statements Elias Hicks added: "I have spoken; and I leave it for the people to judge—I do not assume the judgment seat."

It may be informing in this connection to examine this sermon somewhat in detail, to see if we can find the definite doctrine which aroused the public opposition. The text was, "Let love be without dissimulation." Having declared that there could be no agreement between hatred and love; and that love could not promote discord, he indulged in what may be called a spiritual figure of speech, declaring that a Christian must be in the same life, and live with the same blood that Christ did, making the following explanation: "As the support of the animal life is the blood; so it is with the soul; the breath of life which God breathed into it is the blood of the soul; the life of the soul; and in this sense we are to understand it, and in no other sense."

He referred to the reprover of our sins, said that it is God who reproves us. "Now, here is the great business of our lives," he remarked, "not only to know this reprover, but to know that it is a gift from God, a manifestation of his own pure life, that was in his son Jesus Christ." Continuing he said:

"As the apostle testifies: 'In him was life, and the life

was the light of men; and that was the true light, which lighteth every man that cometh into the world.' Now can we hesitate a single moment, in regard to the truth of this declaration? No sensible, reflecting mind can possibly do it."[2]

Touching the outward and written as compared with the inner law of life, he affirmed:

"Here is a law more comprehensive than the law of Moses, and it is clear to every individual of us, as the law was to the Israelites. For I dare not suppose that the Almighty would by any means make it a doubtful or mysterious one. It would not become God at all to suppose this the case—it would be casting a deep reflection upon his goodness and wisdom. Therefore I conceive that the law written in the heart, if we attend to it and do not turn from it to build up traditions, or depend on anything that arises from self, or that is in our own power, but come to be regulated by this law, we shall see that it is the easiest thing to be understood that can be, and that all our benefits depend on our complying with this law.

"Here now we see what tradition is. It is a departure from this law; and it has the same effect now that tradition had upon the followers of the outward law; as a belief in tradition was produced they were bound by it, and trusted in it. And so people, nowadays, seem to be compelled to believe in tradition, and thus they turn away from the gospel dispensation, or otherwise the light and life of God's Spirit in the soul, which is the law of the new covenant; for the law is light and the commandment a lamp to show us the way to life."[3]

Using the term, "washed clean in the blood of the lamb," he proceeded to explain himself as follows:

"And what is the blood of the lamb? It was his life, my friends; for as outward, material blood was made use of to express the animal life, inspired men used it as a simile. Outward blood is the life of the animal, but it has nothing to do with the soul; for the soul has no animal blood, no material blood. The life of God in the soul is

---

[2] "The Quaker," Vol. I, p. 51.

[3] "The Quaker," Vol. I, p. 61.

the blood of the soul, and the life of God is the blood of
God; and so it was the life and blood of Jesus Christ his
son. For he was born of the spirit of his heavenly Father,
*and swallowed up fully and completely in his divine nature,
so that he was completely divine.* It was this that operated, in that twofold state, and governed the whole animal
man which was the son of Abraham and David—a tabernacle for his blessed soul. Here now we see that flesh and
blood are not capable of being in reality divine; for are they
not altogether under the direction and guidance of the soul?
This the animal body of Jesus did nothing but what the
divine power in the soul told it to do. Here he was
swallowed up in the divinity of his Father while here on
earth, and it was this that was the active thing, the active
principle, that governed the animate earth. For it corre-
sponds, and cannot do otherwise, with Almighty goodness,
that the soul should have power to command the animal
body to do good or evil; because he has placed us in this
probationary state, and in his wisdom has set evil and good
before us—light and darkness. He has made us free
agents, and given us opportunity to make our own election.

"Here now we shall see what is meant by election, the
election of God. We see that those who choose the Lord
for their portion and the God of Jacob for the lot of their
inheritance, these are the elect. And nothing ever did or
can elect a soul to God, but in this choice." [4]

It is not easy to see how any one can impartially consider the foregoing, especially the words printed in *italics,*
and continue to claim that Elias Hicks denied the divinity
of Christ. Near the end of this sermon we find the following paragraph:

"I say, dearly beloved, my soul craves it for us, that
we may sink down and examine ourselves; according to the
declaration of the apostle: 'Examine yourselves whether
ye be in the faith; prove your own selves: know ye not
your own selves, how that Jesus Christ is in you except ye
be reprobates?' Now we cannot suppose that the apostle
meant that outward man that walked about the streets of
Jerusalem; because he is not in any of us. But what is
this Jesus Christ? He came to be a Saviour to that na-

---

tion, and was limited to that nation. He came to gather up, and look up the lost sheep of the house of Israel. But as he was a Saviour in the outward sense, so he was an outward shadow of good things to come; and so the work of the man, Jesus Christ, was a figure. He healed the sick of their outward calamities—he cleansed the leprosy—all of which was external and affected only their bodies—as sickness does not affect the souls of the children of men, though they may labour under all these things. But as he was considered a Saviour, he meant by what he said, a Saviour is within you, the anointing of the spirit of God is within you; for this made the ways of Jesus so wonderful in his day that the Psalmist in his prophecy concerning him exclaims: 'Thou hast loved righteousness and hated iniquity; therefore God, even thy God hath anointed thee with the oil of gladness above thy fellows.' He had loved righteousness, you perceive, and therefore was prepared to receive the fullness of the spirit, the fullness of that divine anointing; for there was no germ of evil in him or about him; both his soul and body were pure. He was anointed above all his fellows, to be the head of the church, the top stone, the chief corner stone, elect and precious. And what was it that was a Saviour? Not that which was outward; it was not flesh and blood; for 'flesh and blood cannot inherit the kingdom of heaven'; it must go to the earth from whence it was taken. It was that life, that same life that I have already mentioned, that was in him, and which is the light and life of men, and which lighteth every man, and consequently every woman, that cometh into the world. And we have this light and life in us; which is what the apostle meant by Jesus Christ; and if we have not this ruling in us we are dead, because we are not under the law of the spirit of life. For the 'law is light and the reproofs of instruction the way to life.'"[5]

Unless the so-called heterodox doctrine can be found in the foregoing extracts, it does not exist in the sermon under discussion.

Two other sermons were evidently both considered offensive and objectionable by the orthodox. One was preached at the Twelfth Street meeting, Twelfth month 10,

[5] "The Quaker," Vol. I, p. 68.

1826, and the other the 12th of the same month at Key's
Alley, both in Philadelphia. At the Twelfth Street meeting, amid much confusion, Thomas Wistar attempted to
controvert what Elias Hicks had said in certain particulars.
While this Friend was talking, Elias tried to persuade the
audience to be quiet.

At Key's Alley, when Elias had finished, Philadelphia
Pemberton, in the midst of a disturbance that nearly
drowned his voice, gave an exhortation in support of the
outward and vicarious atonement. When Friend Pemberton ceased, Elias Hicks expressed his ideas regarding gospel order and variety in the ministry, for which Friends had
always stood, in which he said:

"My dear friends, God is a God of order—and it will do
me great pleasure to see this meeting sit quiet till it closes.
We have, and claim gospel privileges, and that every one
may be persuaded in his own mind; and as we have gifts
differing, so ought every one to have an opportunity to
speak, one by one, but not two at once, that all may be comforted. If any thing be revealed (and we are not to speak
except this is the case), if any thing be revealed to one,
let others hold their peace—this is according to order.
And I desire it, once for all, my dear friends, if you love
me, that you will keep strictly to this order: it will be a
great comfort to my spirit." [6]

Speaking of the fear of God, he said that he did not
mean "a fear that arises from the dread of torment, or
of chastisement, or anything of this kind: for that may be
no more than the fear of devils, for they, we read, believe
and tremble." His theory was that fear must be based on
knowledge, and the fear to displease God is not because of
what he may do to us, but what, for want of this knowledge,
we lose.

Again, he practically repeated what was evidently con-

---

sidered a truism: 'My friends we are not to look for a law in our neighbor's heart, nor in our neighbor's book; but we are to look for that law which is to be our rule and guide, in our consciences, in our souls; for the law is whole and perfect." Continuing he remarked:

"Now, how concordant this is with the testimony of Jesus, when he queried with his disciples in this wise: 'Whom do men say that I the son of man am?' They enumerated several characters, according to the views of the people in that day. But until we come to this inward, divine law, we shall know nothing rightly of that manifestation; for none of us have seen him, nor any of his works which he acted outwardly. But here we find some are guessing, one way, and some another way, till they become cruel respecting different opinions about him, insomuch that they will kill and destroy each other for their opinions. This is the effect of men's turning away from the true light, the witness for God in their own souls; it throws them into anarchy and confusion."[7]

In the opinion of Elias Hicks, it was not the man Peter that was to constitute the rock upon which the church was to be built, but rather the inner revelation, which enabled the disciple to know that the Master was the Christ. "When a true Christian comes to this rock, he comes to know it, as before pointed out; and here every one must see, when they build on this divine rock, this revealed will of our Heavenly Father, there is no fear."

Touching the vital matters of salvation, we take the following extracts from this sermon:

"Nothing but that which is begotten in every soul can manifest God to the soul. You must know this for yourselves, as nothing which you read in the Scriptures can give you a sense of his saving and almighty power. Now, the only begotten is what the power of God begets in the soul, by the soul uniting with the visitations of divine love.

It becomes like a union—the soul submits and yields itself
up to God and the revelation of his power, and thus it becomes wedded to him as its heavenly husband. Here, now,
is a birth of the Son of God; and this must be begotten in
every soul, as God can be manifested by nothing else.

"Now, what was this Holy Ghost and spirit of truth,
and where are we to find it? He did not leave his disciples
in the dark—'He dwelleth with you, and shall be in you.'
Mind it, my friends. What a blessed sovereign God this
is to be the children of men—a God who has placed a portion of himself in every rational soul—a measure of his
grace sufficient for every purpose, for the redemption of the
souls of men from sin and transgression, and to lead them
to the kingdom of heaven. And there is no other way.
Then do not put it off any longer; do not procrastinate any
longer; do not say to-morrow, but immediately turn inward,
for the day calls aloud for it—everything around us calls
for us to turn inward, to that which will help us to do the
great work of our salvation." [8]

There seems to have been little, if any, public demonstration against the preaching of Elias Hicks in meetings
where he was present, except in Philadelphia. That is especially true before the coming of the English preachers, and
the strained conditions that existed just preceding and during the various acts of separation. It will thus be seen
that the concern and purpose of the ten men elders of Philadelphia remained persistent until the end.

---

[8] "The Quaker," Vol. I, p. 97-98.

The Braithwaite Controversy.

ONE of the marked incidents during the "separation" period was the controversy between Elias Hicks and Anna Braithwaite,[1] and the still more pointed discussion indulged in by the friends and partisans of these two Friends. From our viewpoint there seems to have been a certain amount of unnecessary sensitiveness, which led both these Friends to exalt to the dignity of an insult, and positive impeachment of integrity, matters which probably belonged in the domain of misunderstanding. It was apparently impossible for either to think in the terms of the other, and so the contest went on and ended.

We shall let her friends state the beginning and progress of Anna Braithwaite's religious labor in America, and quote as follows: "She arrived in New York in Eighth month, 1823. For seven months she met with no opposition. True, she always preached orthodox doctrines, but

---

[1] Anna Braithwaite, daughter of Charles and Mary Lloyd, of Birmingham, England, was born Twelfth month, 1788. She was married to Isaac Braithwaite, Third month 26, 1809, and removed to Kendal immediately after. She sailed for America on her first visit, Seventh month 7th, 1823. She attended three meetings in New York, and then the Quarterly Meeting at Burlington, at which place she seems to have been the guest of Stephen Grellet. She made two other visits to America, one in 1825 and the other in 1827. She returned to England after her first visit to America in the autumn of 1824. The last two visits she made to America she was accompanied by her husband. Anna Braithwaite was a woman of commanding presence, and was unusually cultured for one of her sex at that time. She was something of a linguist, speaking several languages. Her visits in America were quite extensive, taking her as far south as North Carolina. She died Twelfth month 18th, 1859.

she had made no pointed allusions to the reputed sentiments of Elias Hicks." [2]

It is interesting to note that the positive preaching of "orthodox doctrine," on its merits, caused no opposition, even from the friends of Elias Hicks, the trouble only coming when a personal application was made, amounting to personal criticism. This is a fine testimony to the ministerial liberty in the Society, and really a confirmation of the claim that spiritual unity, and not doctrinal uniformity, was the true basis of fellowship among Friends. We quote again:

"She visited Long Island in the spring, and had some opportunities of conversing with Elias Hicks on religious subjects, and also of hearing him preach. They differed widely in sentiment, upon important doctrines, and she soon had to conclude that his were at variance with the hitherto well-established principles of the Society. With these views, she returned to New York, and, subsequently, about the time of the Yearly Meeting, in May, she considered it an act of duty to warn her hearers against certain specious doctrines, which were gradually spreading, and undermining what she believed to be the 'true faith.'" [3]

It seems that Anna Braithwaite was twice the guest of Elias Hicks in Jericho, dining at his house both times. The first visit was in First month, 1824, and the other in Third month of the same year. They were both good talkers, and apparently expressed themselves with commendable frankness. The subject-matter of these two conversations, however, became material around which a prolonged controversy was waged. Before Anna Braithwaite sailed for

---

[2] "Calumny Refuted; or, Plain Facts *versus* Misrepresentations." Being reply to Pamphlet entitled, 'The Misrepresentations of Anna Braithwaite in Relation to the Doctrines Preached by Elias Hicks,'" etc., p. 2.

[3] The same, p. 6.

England, she wrote a letter to an unnamed Friend in Flushing relative to the interviews with Elias Hicks. The letter was dated Seventh month 16, 1824.

After Anna Braithwaite's departure from this country, the letter referred to, with "Remarks in Reply to Assertions of Elias Hicks," was published and extensively circulated. It bore the following imprint: "Philadelphia: Printed for the Reader, 1824." [4] In this collection was a letter from Ann Shipley, of New York, dated Tenth month 15, 1824, in which she declares she was present "during the conversation between her [Anna Braithwaite] and Elias Hicks. The statement she left was correct." While Ann Shipley's letter was published without her consent, it seemed to fortify the Braithwaite statement, and both were extensively used in an attempt to cast theological odium on the venerable preacher. The possibility that both women might have misunderstood or misinterpreted Elias Hicks does not seem to have entered the minds of the Anti-Hicks partisans.

This particular epistle of Anna Braithwaite does not contain much material not to be found in a subsequent letter with "notes," which will receive later treatment. In her letter she habitually speaks of herself in the third person, and makes this observation: "When at Jericho in the Third month A. B. took tea with E. H. in a social way. She had not been long in the house, when he began to speak on the subject of the trinity, which A. B. considers a word so grossly abused as to render it undesirable even to make use of it." [5] One cannot well suppress the remark that if a like tenacity of purpose regarding other theological terms had been held and followed by all parties to the controversy,

---

[4] Most of the controversial pamphlets and articles of the "separation" period were anonymous. Except when the articles were printed in regular periodicals, their publishers were as unknown as their authors.

[5] "Remarks in Reply to Assertions of Elias Hicks," p. 7.

the history of the Society of Friends would have been entirely different from the way it now has to be written.

Touching the two visits to Elias Hicks, we have direct testimony from the visitor. We quote:

"I thought on first entering the house, my heart and flesh would fail, but after a time of inexpressible conflict, I felt a consoling belief that best help would be near, and I think that every opposing thing was in a great measure kept down. . . . He listened to my views, which I was enabled to give with calmness. He was many times brought into close quarters; but when he could not answer me directly, he turned to something else. My mind is sorrowfully affected on this subject, and the widespread mischief arising from the propagation of such sentiments."[6]

In another letter, written to her family, she thus referred to her interview with Elias Hicks:

"I have reason to think that, notwithstanding the firm and honest manner in which my sentiments were expressed, an open door is left for further communication. We met in love and we parted in love. He wept like a child for some time before we separated; so that it was altogether a most affecting opportunity."[7]

While these two Friends undoubtedly were present in the same meeting during the subsequent visits of Anna Braithwaite to this country, their relations became so strained that they never met on common Friendly ground after the two occasions mentioned.

After the publication of the communication and comments referred to, Elias Hicks wrote a long letter to his friend, Dr. Edwin A. Atlee, of Philadelphia.[8] This letter became the subject of a good deal of controversy, and may have been the exciting cause of a letter which Anna Braith-

---

[6] "Memoirs of Anna Braithwaite," by her son, J. Bevan Braithwaite, p. 129-130.

[7] The same, p. 140.

[8] The text of this letter will be found listed as Appendix B in this book.

waite wrote Elias Hicks on the 13th of Eleventh month, 1824, from Lodge Lane, near Liverpool. This letter, with elaborate "notes," was published and widely circulated on this side of the ocean. The letter itself would have caused very little excitement, but the "notes" were vigorous causes of irritation and antagonism. The authorship of the "notes" was a matter of dispute. It was claimed that they were not written by Anna Braithwaite, and the internal evidence gave color to that conclusion. They were not, in whole or in part, entirely in her spirit, and the temper of them was rather masculine. There were persons who believed, but, of course, without positive evidence, that Joseph John Gurney was their author.

The letter of Anna Braithwaite contains few points not covered by the "notes." She charges that Elias had denied that the Scriptures were a rule of faith and practice, and it was also claimed that he repudiated "the propitiatory sacrifice of our Lord and Savior Jesus Christ." This, she affirmed, was infidelity of a most pronounced type.

The "notes" attached to this letter constitute a stinging arraignment of the supposed sentiments of Elias Hicks. They were considered by his friends such an unwarranted attack as to call for vigorous treatment, and in numerous ways they became points of controversy. They were mild at first, but personal and almost bitter at the last. The first "note" in the collection briefly, but fully, lays the foundation for arbitrary authority in religion. It says:

"It is a regulation indispensably necessary to the peace of society, and to the preservation of order, consistency and harmony among Christians, that the members of every religious body, and especially those who assume the office of teachers or ministers, should be responsible to the authorities established in the church, for the doctrines which they hold and promulgate." [9]

---

[9] A letter from Anna Braithwaite to Elias Hicks, on the Nature of His Doctrines, etc., p. 9.

There is critical reference to a statement which Anna Braithwaite said Elias Hicks made in the Meeting of Ministers and Elders in Jericho, touching spiritual guidance in appointing people to service in the Society. She says that Elias declared that "if each Friend attended to his or her proper gift, as this spirit is endued with prescience, that no Friend would be named for any appointment, but such as would attend, and during my long course of experience, I have never appointed any one who was prevented from attending either by illness or otherwise." [10]

In his letter to Dr. Atlee, Elias states his expression at the meeting as differing from Anna Braithwaite's in a material way. This is what he declares he said: "That I thought there was something wrong in the present instance, for, as we profess to believe in the guidance of the Spirit of Truth as an unerring Spirit, was it not reasonable to expect, especially in a meeting of ministers and elders, that if each Friend attended to their proper gifts, as this Spirit is endued with prescience, that it would be much more likely, under its divine influence, we should be led to appoint such as would attend on particular and necessary occasions, than to appoint those who would not attend?"

We make these quotations not only to show the difference in the two statements, but to also make it plain what small faggots were used to build the fires of controversy regarding the opinions of Elias Hicks. It looks in this particular citation like a case of criticism gone mad. The following extracts are from the "notes":

"We shall now notice the comparatively modern work of that arch-infidel, Thomas Paine, called "The Age of Reason," many of the sentiments of which are so exactly similar to those of Elias Hicks, as almost to induce us to suspect plagiarism." [11]

---

[10] The same, p. 4.

[11] The same, p. 23-24.

"We could adduce large quotations from authors of the same school with Paine, showing in the most conclusive manner that the dogmas of Elias Hicks, so far from being further revelations of Christian doctrines, are merely the stale objections to the religion of the Bible, which have been so frequently routed and driven from the field, to the utter shame and confusion of their promulgators." [12]

Those who defended Elias Hicks saw in these criticisms an act of persecution, and a veiled attempt to undermine his reputation as a man and a minister. The latter effort was read into the following paragraph, which was presented as an effort at justifying the criticism of the Jericho preacher. We quote:

"It was both Friendly and Christian to warn them of the danger of listening with credulity to one whose high profession, reputed morality, and popular eloquence, had given him considerable influence; and if his opinions had been correct, the promulgation of them would not have proved prejudicial to him." [13]

The references to Thomas Paine will sound singularly overdrawn if read in connection with the reference of Elias Hicks to the same person. [14] It may be asserted with some degree of safety that it is doubtful if either Elias Hicks or his critics ever read enough of the writings of Thomas Paine to be really qualified to judicially criticise them.

When Anna Braithwaite visited this country the second time, in 1825, she found matters much more unsettled than on her first visit. Her own part in the controversy had been fully, if not fairly, discussed. As showing her own feeling touching the second visit, we quote the following from a sermon preached by her:

"I have thought many times, while surrounded by my

[12] The same, p. 26.

[13] The same, p. 21-22.

[14] See page 117 of this book.

family and my friends, and when I have bowed before the
throne of grace, how very near and how very dear were
my fellow-believers, on this side of the Atlantic, made unto
my soul. It seemed to me, as if in a very remarkable manner, their everlasting welfare was brought before me, as if
my fellow-professors of the same religious principles with
myself were in a very peculiar manner the objects of much
solicitude. How have I had to pour out my soul in secret
unto the Lord, that he would turn them more and more,
and so let their light shine before men, that all being
believers in a crucified Saviour, they may be brought to
know for themselves that though 'Christ Crucified was to
the Jews a stumbling block, and unto the Greeks foolish-
ness; but unto them which are called, both Jews and Greeks,
Christ, the power of God and the wisdom of God.' I say
my soul hath been poured out before the Lord, that their
light might shine in a still more conspicuous manner,
through their hearts being brought into deep prostration of
soul, that so their works might glorify their Father which is
in heaven. My heart was enlarged toward every religious
denomination; for surely, the world over, those who are
believers in Christ have one common bond of union—they
are the salt of the earth—the little flock to whom the Father
in his good pleasure will give the Kingdom. I have often
greatly desired to be with you, while I am well aware that
to many it must appear a strange thing, that a female
should leave her home, her family, and her friends, and
should thus expose herself to the public, to preach the glad
tidings of salvation through Jesus Christ; yet I have
thought, my beloved friends, that though all may not see
into these things, yet surely there is no other way for any
of us, but to yield up our thoughts unto the Lord." [15]

There seem to have been some Friends desirous of
producing a meeting between Anna Braithwaite and Elias
Hicks during this visit. In Tenth month, 1825, she wrote
him from Kipp's Bay, Long Island. She informed him of
her arrival, and then stated "that if he wishes to have any
communication with her, she is willing to meet him in the
presence of their mutual friends, or to answer any letter he

[15] Sermon and prayer by Anna Braithwaite, delivered in Friends'
Meeting, Arch Street, Philadelphia, October 26, 1825. Taken in short-
hand by M. T. C. Gould, stenographer, p. 4-5.

may write to her;" then she adds these remarkable words:
'Having written to thee sometime ago, what I thought was
right, I do not ask an interview.' " [16]

To this communication Elias Hicks made a somewhat
full reply. He says that her notes of the conversation,
"divers of which were without foundation," led him to
wonder why she should even think of having any future
communication with him. He then says:

"That I have no desire for any further communication
with thee, either directly or indirectly, until thou makest
a suitable acknowledgment for thy breach of friendship, as
is required by the salutary discipline of our Society; but as
it respects myself, I freely forgive thee, and leave thee to
pursue thy own way as long as thou canst find true peace
and quiet therein." [17]

It has to be said regretfully that during Anna Braithwaite's second visit to this country, she met with both
personal and Society rebuffs. In some meetings her minute
was read, but with no expression of approbation in the case.
The Meeting of Ministers and Elders at Jericho appointed
a committee,[18] to advise her not to appoint any more meetings in that neighborhood during her stay. A good many
Friends objected to her family visits, and, taken altogether,
her stay must have been one of trial.

She came again in the early part of the year 1827,
and was here when the climax came in that year and the
year following.

The English Friends, who were so much in evidence
in our troubles, went home to face the Beacon controversy.[19]

---

[16] "Christian Inquirer," new series, Vol. 1., 1826, p. 57.

[17] The same, p. 57.

[18] The same, p. 59.

[19] This controversy took its name from a periodical call the "Beacon," edited by Isaac Crewdson. In this evangelical doctrines and

their gathering in England. The Beaconite movement caused several hundred Friends to sever their connection with the Society. But it did not reach the dignity of a division or a separation. Whether the English Friends profited by the experiences suffered by the Society in America is not certain. At any rate, they seem to have been able to endure their differences without a rupture.

After the English trouble had practically subsided, in 1841, Anna Braithwaite made the following suggestive admission, which may well close this chapter:

"Calm reflection and observation of passing events, and of persons, have convinced me that I took an exaggerated view of the state of society with reference to Hicksism . . . We have as great a horror of Hicksism as ever, but we think Friends generally are becoming more alive to its dangers, and that the trials of the last few years have been blessed to the instruction of many." [20]

---

methods were advocated. The Beaconites were strong in advocating the doctrine of justification by faith, and practically rejected the fundamental Quaker theory of the Inner Light. From the American standpoint, the Beaconite position seems to have been the logical development of the doctrines preached by the English and American opponents of Elias Hicks.

[20] "J. Bevan Braithwaite: a Friend of the Nineteenth Century," by his children, p. 59-60.

CHAPTER XIX.

Ann Jones in Dutchess County.

In Fifth month, 1828, a year after the division had been accomplished in Philadelphia, a most remarkable round of experiences took place within the bounds of Nine Partners and Stanford Quarterly Meetings, in Dutchess County, New York. Elias Hicks was past eighty years of age, but he attended the series of meetings in the neighborhood mentioned. George and Ann Jones, English Friends, much in evidence in "separation" matters, were also in attendance, the result being a series of controversial exhortations, mingled with personal allusions, sometimes gently veiled, but containing what would now pass for bitterness and railing. The "sermons" of this series were stenographically reported, and form a small book of ninety-eight pages.

The first meeting was held at Nine Partners, First-day, Fifth month 4th. Elias Hicks had the first service in the meeting. After he had closed, Ann Jones made the following remarks:

"We have heard considerable said, and we have heard, under a specious pretence of preaching the Gospel, the Saviour of the world denied, who is God and equal with the Father. And we have heard that the Scriptures had done more hurt than good. We have also heard the existence of a devil denied, except what arises from our propensities, desires, &c."[1]

---

[1] "Sermons" by Elias Hicks, Ann Jones and others of the Society of Friends, at the Quarterly Meeting of Nine Partners and Stanford, and first day preceding in Fifth month, 1828. Taken in shorthand by Henry Hoag, p. 20.

After this deliverance, Elias Hicks again arose and said:

"I will just observe that my friends are acquainted with me in these parts, and know me very well when I speak to them. I came not here as a judge, but as a counsellor: I leave it for the people to judge. And I would hope to turn them to nothing but a firm and solid conviction in their minds. We may speak one by one, for that becometh order. I thought I would add a word or two more. When I was young, I read the Scriptures, and I thought that they were not the power, nor the spirit, and that there was but very little in them for me; but I was vain. But when I had once seen the sin in my heart, then I found that this book pointed to the Spirit, but never convicted me of sin.

"I believe that this was the doctrine of ancient Friends; for George Fox declared that his Saviour never could be slain by the hands of wicked men. I believe the Scriptures concerning Jesus Christ, and David, too, and a host of others, who learned righteousness and were united one with another. I believe that Jesus Christ took upon him flesh made under the law, for all people are made under the law, and Christ is this Light which enlighteneth every man that comes into the world. And now, my friends, I would not have you believe one word of what I say, unless by solid conviction." [2]

It will be in order to find out what was said by Elias Hicks which called for the personal allusion made by Ann Jones. We are not able to find in the remarks of Elias Hicks on this occasion anything that would justify the strong language of his critic, especially as to the Scriptures having done more hurt than good. It would seem that the supplementary statement quoted must be accepted as containing his estimate of the book which he was charged with repudiating, rather than the critical assertion of his doctrinal opponent.

There are various statements in the Hicks sermon which denied some of the material claims of popular

---

[2] The same.

theology, but they did not class him with those who denied the existence or spiritual office of Christ. In the meetings under review, and at other times, the evidence is abundant that his critics either did not want to or could not understand him. He dealt with the spirit of the gospel, and with the inner manifestation of that spirit in the heart. They stood for scriptural literalness, and for the outward appearance of Christ. It is not for us to condemn either side in the controversy, but to state the case.

We produce a few sentences and expressions from the sermon by Elias Hicks, which might have created antagonism at the time. Speaking of the "Comforter" which was to come, he said:

"And what was this Comforter? Not an external one— not Jesus Christ outward, to whom there was brought diseased persons and he delivered them from their various diseases. . . . Here, now, he told them how to do: he previously made mention that when the Comforter had come, he would reprove the world of sin—now the world is every rational soul under heaven. And he has come and reproved them. I dare appeal to the wickedest man present, that will acknowledge the truth, that this Light has come into the world; but men love darkness better than light, because their deeds are evil; yet they know the light by an evidence in their hearts." [3]

Near the end of this discourse he elaborated his idea as to the ineffectual character of all outward and formal soul cleansing, in the following language:

"Now can any man of common sense suppose that it can be outward blood that was shed by the carnal Jews that will cleanse us from our sins? The blood of Chirst that is immortal, never can be seen by mortal eyes. And to be Christians, we must come to see an immortal view. After Chirst had recapitulated the precepts of the law, 'Is it not written in your law, an eye for an eye, and a tooth for a

[3] The same, p. 9.

tooth : but I say unto you, if any smite thee on one cheek turn to him the other also: and if any take thy coat from thee, give him thy cloak also.' Don't we see how different the precepts of the law of God are? He tells us how we should do—we should take no advantage at all. The Almighty visits us, to get us willing to observe his law; and if all were concerned to maintain his law, all lawyers would be banished; we should have no need of them; as well as of hireling Priests. We should have no need of them to teach us, nor no need of the laws of men, for each one would have a law in his own mind." [4]

The other points in Dutchess County visited, and involved in the reports of sermons under consideration, were Chestnut Ridge, Stanford and Oblong. At some of these meetings the preachers spoke more than once. It does not appear that in the brief communications of George Jones he either directly or indirectly referred to statements made by Elias Hicks, or particularly sought to antagonize them. Ann Jones, however, was not similarly considerate and cautious. Either directly or by inference, she quite generally attempted to furnish the antidote for what she considered the pernicious doctrine of her fellow-minister. Speaking at Nine Partners Quarterly Meeting, Fifth month 7th, she said:

"I believe it to be right for me to caution the present company without respect of persons—how they deny the Lord that bought them—how they set at nought the outward coming of the Lord Jesus Christ who died for them : they will have to answer it at the awful tribunal bar of God. where it will be altogether unavailing to say that such a one taught me to believe that there was nothing in this. Oh! my friends! God hath not left us without a witness: Oh, then it is unto the faithful and true witness, 'the testimony of Jesus, which is the spirit of prophecy.' I am engaged in gospel love to recommend, and to hold out unto you, that you meddle not with the things of God; and that you cry unto him for help. For what hope can they have

' The same, p. 17.

of present or future good, or of everlasting happiness, if they reject the only means appointed of God to come unto the Father through Jesus Christ, the messenger of God, and of the new covenant?" [5]

At this meeting Elias Hicks followed Ann Jones in vocal communication. He made no direct reference to what she said, the short sermon being largely a reiteration touching the inner revelation to the souls of men, as the reprover of sin, and the power which kept from sinning. as against the outward, sacrificial form of salvation. In closing his remarks, Elias Hicks made this statement:

"I do not wish to detain this assembly much longer, but I want that we should cast away things that are mysterious, for we cannot comprehend mystery. 'Secret things belong to God, but those that are revealed (that are understood), to us and our children.' And those that are secret can never be found out by the prying of mortals. Do we suppose for a moment—for it would cast an indignity upon God to suppose that he had laid down any name except his own by which we can have communion with him. It is a plain way, a simple way which all can understand, and not be under the necessity to go to a neighbor, and to say, 'Know thou the Lord? for all shall know me, from the least of them unto the greatest of them,' as said Jeremy the prophet. It is bowing down to an ignorant state of mind, to suppose that there is no other power whereby we can come unto God, but by one of the offspring of Abraham, and that we have need to go back to the law which was given to the Israelites, and to no other people. He has never made any covenant with any other people, but that which he made with our first parents. That is the covenant that has been made with all the nations of the earth.

"He justifies for good and condemns for evil. And although every action is to be from the operation of his power, yet he has given us the privilege to obey or disobey; here now is a self-evident truth; as they have the liberty to choose, so if they do that which is contrary to his will, and so slay the Divine life in the soul: and thus they have slain the innocent Lamb of God in the soul, which is the same thing. All that we want, is to return to the inward

light in the soul. The Lord had declared beforehand unto
them in plain characters, that none need to say, 'Know ye
the Lord? for I will be merciful to them, I will forgive their
iniquity, and I will remember their sin no more.' This
was equally the case until the law was abolished: until he
blotted out the handwriting of the law, and put an end to
outward ordinances. The law was fulfilled when they had
crucified him, then it was that that law was abolished that
consisted in making their atonements which all had to make.

"The people could not understand the doctrine delivered in the sermon on the mount, although plainly
preached to them. Jesus, when about to take leave of his
disciples, left this charge with them: 'Tarry at Jerusalem
until the Holy Ghost come upon you'; and then, and not
till then, were they to bear witness unto him. He told
them that it would bring everything to their remembrance:
everything which is by the preaching of the gospel brought
to your remembrance; therefore he says: 'All things shall
be brought to your remembrance.' They would not then
be looking to anything outward, because he had filled them
with the Spirit of truth. What is this, but this Comforter
which reproves the world of sin? All that will obey the
voice of this reprover in the soul are in the way of redemption and salvation. 'By disobedience, sin entered into the
world and death by sin: but life and immortality is brought
to light by the gospel.' I am willing to leave you, and I
recommend you to God, and the power of his grace, which is
able to build you up, as you are faithful to its operation." [6]

The last meeting of the series was held in connection
with Nine Partners Quarterly Meeting, Fifth month 9th.
This was evidently the closing session of the Quarterly
Meeting. From these published sermons it would seem
that Elias Hicks and George Jones were the only Friends
who engaged in vocal ministry that day. There was nothing
specially relevant to the controversy going on in the Society
in either of these short discourses.

In reading this collection of sermons one cannot avoid
the conclusion that, apart from dissimilarity in phraseology,
and the matters involved in interpreting Scripture, these

---

[6] The same, p. 71.

Friends had much in common. Had they been minded to seek for the common ground, it is quite probable that they would have found that they were really quarreling over the minor, rather than the major, propositions.

In Eighth month, 1828, Elias Hicks was on his last religious visit to the Western Yearly Meetings. The "separation" in the New York Yearly Meeting had taken place in Fifth month, the trouble then passing to the Quarterly and particular meetings. It reached Nine Partners at the Quarterly Meeting held as above. Ann Jones attended this meeting, the last sermon in the little volume from which the extracts given in this chapter are taken having been preached by this Friend. There was little new matter in this sermon. Much, by innuendo, was laid at the door of those who were pronounced unorthodox, and who constituted a majority of the meeting.

So far as the charge of persecution is concerned, it was repeatedly employed by Elias Hicks and his sympathizers in describing the spirit and conduct of the orthodox party. In this particular, at least, the disputants on both sides were very much alike. Ann Jones' reference to throwing down "his elders and prophets" contains more touching the animus of the controversy than the few words really indicate. As will be somewhat clearly shown in these pages, the trouble in the Society quite largely had reference to authority in the church, and its arbitrary exercise by a select few, constituting a sort of spiritual and social hierarchy in the monthly meetings. It was this authoritative class which had been "thrown down," or was likely to be so repudiated.

We would by no means claim that with the "separation" an accomplished fact, the body of Friends not of the orthodox party thus gathered by themselves became at once and continuously relieved of the arbitrary spirit. The history of this branch of the Society from 1827 to 1875, and in places down to date, would entirely disprove any such claim. It would seem that wherever the Society lost ground numerically, and wherever its spiritual life dwindled, it was due largely because some sort of arbitrary authority ignored the necessity for real spiritual unity, and discounted the spiritual democracy upon which the Society of Friends was based.

The "separation" in the Quarterly Meetings in Dutchess County was perfected in Eighth month, 1828. Both Anna Braithwaite and Ann Jones were in attendance, and evidently took part in the developments at that time. Elias Hicks was on his last religious visit to the "far west." Informing partnership letters were sent to Elias, then in Mt. Pleasant, Ohio, by Jacob and Deborah Willetts,[8] under date of Eighth month 18, 1828. Jacob gave brief but explicit information as to the division in the several meetings. For instance, he says that in Oswego Monthly Meeting one-sixth of the members went orthodox. At Creek, about one-fourth left to form an orthodox meeting, about the same proportion existing at Stanford. Nine Partners seems to have been the center of the difficulty, the orthodox leadership apparently having been more vigorous at that point. Still, about three-fourths of the members refused to join the orthodox. A very brief appreciation of the transatlantic visitors is given in Jacob's letter. He says: "The English Friends are very industrious, but I do not find that

---

[8] Jacob and Deborah Willetts were friendly educators in the first half of the nineteenth century. Jacob became principal of Nine Partners boarding school in 1803, when only 18 years of age, and Deborah Rogers principal of the girl's department in 1806, when at the same age. Jacob Willetts and Deborah Rogers were married in 1812. At the time of the "separation," Nine Partners' school passed into the hands of the Orthodox, and Jacob and Deborah resigned their positions, and started a separate school, which they conducted successfully for nearly thirty years. Jacob was the author of elementary text books of arithmetic and geography, and Deborah was an accomplished grammarian, and assisted Gould Brown in the preparation of his once well-known English Grammar.

it amounts to much. Friends have generally become acquainted with their manœuvring."

Deborah's letter was both newsy and personal, and threw interesting sidelights on the "separation" experiences. At the close of a sermon by Ann Jones, Eighth month 5th, she made reference to the sudden death of a woman Friend of the orthodox party, which is thus referred to in this letter:

"Perhaps thou wilt hear ere this reaches thee of the death of Ann Willis. She died at William Warings on her way home from Purchase Quarterly Meeting, in an apoplectic fit. At our Quarterly Meeting Ann Jones told us of the dear departed spirit of one who had lived an unspotted life, who passed away without much bodily suffering, and whose soul was now clothed in robes of white, singing glory, light and majesty with angels forever and ever: which amounted nearly to a funeral song."

We make the following extract from the letter of Deborah Willetts because of its interesting references and statements:

"A week ago I returned from Stanford Quarterly Meeting held at Hudson. All the English force was there save T. Shillitoe with a large re-enforcement from New York, but they were headed by 15 men and 25 women of the committee of Friends, and a great many attended from the neighboring meetings, Coeymans, Rensalaerville, Saratoga, &c. The city was nearly full. Anna Braithwaite and suite took lodgings at the hotel. It was the most boisterous meeting I ever attended. The clerks in each meeting were orthodox, but Friends were favored to appoint others who opened the meeting. Anna Braithwaite had much to say to clear up the charges against her in circulation that their expenses had been borne by Friends, which she said was false, and never had been done but in two instances, and mentioned it twice or three times that her dear husband felt it a very great pleasure to meet all expenses she might incur, and she would appeal to those present for the truth of what she had said, and then Ann Jones, Claussa Griffin, Ruth Hallock, Sarah Upton and some others immediately attested to the truth of it. Oh, how inconsistent is all this in a Friends' meeting. She also gave a long statement of the separation at Yearly Meeting, but she was reminded of her absence at the time, but she replied Ann Jones had informed her. She accused Friends of holding erroneous doctrine and said Phebe I. Merritt did not believe in the atonement for sin. Phebe said she denied the charge, when Anna turning and looking stern in her face said, 'Did thou not say, Phebe Merritt, all the reproof thou felt for sin was in thy own breast?' Phebe then arose and was favored to express her views in a clear way with an affecting circumstance that she experienced in her childhood that brought such a solemnity over the meeting that almost disarmed Anna of her hostile proceedings. She stood upon her feet the while ready to reply but began in a different tone of voice, and changed the subject, and very soon after, Ann Jones made a move to adjourn when they could hold Stanford Quarterly Meeting, which was seconded by several others and Friends in the meantime as cordially and silently uniting with them in the motion. They then retired without reading an adjournment, I afterwards learnt, to the Presbyterian Conference room. I dined in company with Willett Hicks, who said he was surprised to see so few go with them after such a noble effort."

CHAPTER XX.

The Experience with T. Shillitoe.

THE first day after his arrival in America, Thomas Shillitoe [1] attended Hester Street Meeting, in New York. He tells that "it was reported that he had come over to help the Friends of Elias Hicks." [2] As this Friend came into collision with Elias several times, and was second to none in vigor and virulence among his antagonists, either domestic or foreign, it seems proper to review his connection with the controversy, because some added light may thus be thrown on the spirit and purpose of the opposition to Elias Hicks.

Of the experience on that first meeting in America the venerable preacher says: "I found it hard work to rise upon my feet, but believing that the offer of the best of all help was made, I ventured and was favored to clear my mind faithfully, and in a manner I apprehended would give such of the followers of Elias Hicks as were present a pretty clear idea of the mistake they had been under of my being come over to help their unchristian cause." [3]

He had not been seen at that time to converse with a

---

[1] Thomas Shillitoe was born in London "about the Second month, 1754," Elias Hicks being six years his senior. His parents were not Friends. At one time his father kept an inn. Joined Grace Church Street Monthly Meeting in London about 1775. Was acknowledged a minister at Tottenham in 1790. He learned the grocery business, and afterward entered a banking house. Finally learned shoemaker's trade, and had a shop. Was married in 1778. Came to America in 1826, arriving in New York, Ninth month 8th. While here traveled extensively, visiting certain Indian tribes. In 1827 he had an interview with President Andrew Jackson. He left New York for Liverpool in Eighth month, 1829, having been in this country nearly three years. Thomas Shillitoe died in 1836.

[2] "Journal of Thomas Shillitoe," Vol 2, p. 150.

[3] "Journal of Thomas Shillitoe," Vol. 2, p. 151.

single friend of Elias Hicks, and there is no evidence that during the three years he was in America he mingled at all with any Friends who were not of the so-called orthodox party.

During the week following his arrival in this country, Thomas Shillitoe visited Jericho by way of Westbury. Regarding his visit he says:

"We took our dinner with G. Seaman; after which we proceeded to Jericho, and took up our abode this night with our kind friend, Thomas Willis. In passing through the village of Jericho, Elias Hicks was at his own door; he invited me into his own house to take up my abode, which I found I could not have done, even had we not previously concluded to take up our abode with T. Willis. I refused his offer in as handsome a manner as I well knew how. He then pressed me to make him a call; I was careful to make such a reply as would not make it binding upon me, although we had to pass his door on our way to the next meeting. I believe it was safest for me not to comply with his request." [4]

G. Seaman, mentioned above, became the first clerk of the Orthodox Monthly Meeting of Westbury and Jericho, organized after the "separation," and Thomas Willis was the Friend who should probably be called the father of the opposition to Elias Hicks. Had the English visitor determined from the start to hear nothing, and know nothing but one side of the controversy, he could not have more fully made that possible than by the intercourse he had with Friends on this continent.

To show how bent he was not to be influenced or contaminated by those not considered orthodox, it may be noted that while in Jericho he was visited by Friends in that neighborhood, who urged him to call on them. He was at first inclined to acquiesce, but after "waiting where the divine counsellor is to be met with," he changed his mind.

remarking, "I afterwards understood some of these individuals were of Elias Hicks's party." [5]

The New York Yearly Meeting of 1827 was attended by all of the ministering Friends and their companions from England, viz: Thomas Shillitoe, Elizabeth Robson, George and Ann Jones, Isaac and Anna Braithwaite. There seems to have been a foreshadowing of trouble in this yearly meeting. Elizabeth Robson asked for a minute to visit men's meeting, which met with some opposition, and was characterized by confusion in carrying out the purpose. Elias Hicks says nothing about the matter in his Journal, and no reference was made to this Friend in his personal correspondence. The English Friends left New York before the close of the Yearly Meeting, to attend New England Yearly Meeting.

It is not our purpose to follow the wanderings of Thomas Shillitoe in America. He was at the New York Yearly Meeting again in 1828, at the time of the "separation." Touching this occasion, the minutes of the meeting in question furnish some information, as follows: "Thomas Shillitoe, who is in this country on a religious visit from England, objected to the company of some individuals who were present with us, and members of a neighboring yearly meeting, stating that they had been regularly disowned," etc. [6] For thus dictating to the yearly meeting, Thomas Shillitoe presented this justification:

"I obtained a certificate from my own monthly meeting and quarterly meeting, and also one from the Select Yearly Meeting of Friends held in London, expressive of their concurrence with my traveling in the work of the ministry on this continent, which certificates were read in the last

[5] "Journal of Thomas Shillitoe," Vol. 2, p. 154.

[6] From Minute Book of New York Yearly Meeting, session of 1828.

Yearly Meeting of New York, and entered in the records of that Yearly Meeting; such being the case, it constitutes me as much a member of this Yearly Meeting as any other member of it." [6]

This may have been according to good society order and etiquette eighty odd years ago, but would hardly pass current in our time. For a visitor in a meeting to object to the presence of other visitors, on the ground of rumor and with no regular or official evidence of the charges against them, would probably put the objector into disfavor. But we are not warranted in passing harsh judgment in the nineteenth-century case. The English Friends, right or wrong, came to this country under the impression that they were divinely sent to save the Society of Friends in America from going to the bad. At the worst, it was a case of assuming the care of too many consciences.

Soon after the close of the New York Yearly Meeting of 1828, both Thomas Shillitoe and Elias Hicks started on a western trip. Elias seems to have preceded the English Friend by a few days. The two men met at Westland. [7] At this place Thomas says that Elias denied that Jesus was the son of God, until after the baptism, and opposed the proper observance of the Sabbath. [8] Of course, the statements of Elias were controverted by his fellow-preacher, or, at least, an attempt to do so was made. It should be understood that Elias denied that Jesus was the son of God in the sense in which Thomas conceived he was, and he undoubtedly antagonized the observance of the Sabbath in the slavish way which considered that man was secondary to the institution.

Part of the mission of our English Friend from this

---

[6] "Journal of Thomas Shillitoe," Vol. 2, p. 311.

[7] See page 47 of this book.

[8] "Journal of Thomas Shillitoe," Vol. 2, p. 328.

time seems to have been to oppose Elias Hicks, and turn the minds of the people against him. They both attended Redstone Monthly Meeting. Here Elias presented his minute of unity and the other evidences of good faith which he possessed. At this point Thomas says: "Observing a disposition in most of the members of the meeting to have these minutes read in the meeting, I proposed to the meeting to consider how far with propriety they could read them; after their Meeting for Sufferings had given forth a testimony against the doctrines of Elias Hicks. But a determination to read his minutes being manifested, Friends were obliged to submit." [9]

Taken altogether, this is a remarkable statement. The "testimony" referred to was the "declaration of faith" [10] published by the Philadelphia Meeting for Sufferings. This document did not mention Elias Hicks, and failed to secure the approval of the Yearly Meeting, before the "separation." It is evident that "most of the members" were with Elias Hicks on this occasion. Only the few opposers were "Friends"; so the statement infers.

The two preachers are next heard from at Redstone Quarterly Meeting, where Thomas was disposed to practice an act of self-denial. He told the meeting that he preferred his own minute should not be read, if Elias Hicks's was received. We have some evidence from Elias Hicks himself regarding this incident, in a letter written to Valentine and Abigail Hicks, from Pittsburg, Eighth month 5, 1828, stating the proposition of Thomas Shillitoe regarding his minute. Elias says: "Friends took him at his word, and let him know that they should not minute it, but insisted that mine should be minuted, expressing very general satisfaction with my company and service, and reprobated his

---

[9] "Journal of Thomas Shillitoe," Vol. 2, p. 330.
[10] See page 139 of this book.   24

in plain terms, and charged him and his companion with breach of the order and discipline of the Society, and insisted that the elders and overseers should stop at the close of the meeting and see what could be done to put a stop to such disorderly conduct."

Thomas then says that he exposed Elias Hicks as an impostor "in attempting as he did to impose himself upon the public as a minister in unity with the Society of Friends; the Society having, by a printed document, declared against his doctrine, and himself as an approved minister." [11]   Evidently this was another reference to the much-lauded "declaration of faith," although this did not represent an actually authoritative declaration of the Society.   At its best, Philadelphia's Meeting for Sufferings was not the Society of Friends; but the people still wanted to hear Elias.   They apparently preferred to interpret him at first-hand.

Thomas Shillitoe tells us that when they crossed the Ohio River he talked with the woman at the ferry, who protested against the ideas of Elias Hicks, and then remarks: "She kept a tavern, and I left with her one of the declarations, requesting her to circulate it amongst her neighbors." [12]   Evidently the publican, in this case, was sound in the faith as held by the English preacher.

Mt. Pleasant was next visited by both Friends, preceding and at Ohio Yearly Meeting.   They do not seem to have come personally into collision at this point, and insofar as either makes reference to the occurrences there, they are in substantial agreement. [13]   Thomas Shillitoe bears mildly veiled testimony to the desire of the people to hear Elias Hicks, in the following statement: "From the great con-

---

[11] "Journal of Thomas Shillitoe," Vol. 2, p. 331.

[12] "Journal of Thomas Shillitoe," Vol. 2, p. 332.

[13] For other reference to this matter, see page 49 of this book.

course of people we passed in the afternoon on the way
to Short Creek Meeting, where Elias Hicks was to be, I
had cherished a hope we should have had a quiet meeting
at Mt. Pleasant." [14]   But the contrary was the case; to
whom the blame was due, the reader may decide.

It is to be presumed that these two Friends, both of
whom performed valuable service for the Society, according
to their lights and gifts, never met after their western
experience.   For the want of understanding each other,
they went their way not as fellow-servants, but as strangers,
if not enemies.   The unity of the spirit was obliterated in
a demand for uniformity of speculative doctrine.

---

[14] "Journal of Thomas Shillitoe, Vol. 2, p. 343.

CHAPTER XXI.

Disownment and Doctrine.

THE "separation" was accomplished in most meetings in the East by the withdrawal of the orthodox party, after which they set up new meetings for worship and discipline. In a minority of meetings the orthodox held the property and the organization, and the other Friends withdrew. At Jericho and Westbury the great majority of the members remained, and continued to occupy the old meeting-houses. The orthodox who separated from the Westbury and Jericho Monthly Meetings organized the Monthly Meeting of Westbury and Jericho, as has already been mentioned.

In 1829, when the new monthly meeting was formed, the membership of Westbury Monthly Meeting was as follows: Westbury Preparative Meeting, 193; Matinecock Preparative Meeting, 121; Cow Neck (now Manhassett), 65; total, 379. Of this number, accessions to the orthodox were: From Westbury Preparative Meeting, 32; Matinecock Preparative Meeting, 2; Cow Neck Preparative Meeting, 5; total, 39. In Jericho the members of the monthly meeting, Fifth month, 1829, numbered 225. Of this number, nine left to join the Monthly Meeting of Westbury and Jericho, and five were undetermined in their choice. Giving the latter meeting the benefit of the doubt, and assigning to it the five uncertain members, the meeting that disowned Elias Hicks was composed of fifty-three members, of whom thirteen were minors and five of only mild allegiance.

A simple mathematical calculation will show that the

Monthly Meeting of Westbury and Jericho contained 10 per cent. of the Friends who had been members of the two original monthly meetings, which meetings still survived. retaining 90 per cent. of the members. These figures will throw suggestive light on what follows.

It was the Westbury and Jericho Monthly Meeting which, on the 29th of Fourth month, 1829, adopted the "testimony against Elias Hicks," called his disownment. It contained specified charges, which may be condensed as follows: He denied the influence or existence of an evil spirit; doubted the fall of man, and his redemption through Christ; endeavored to "destroy a belief in the miraculous conception of our Lord and Saviour Jesus Christ"; also rejected a "belief in his holy offices, his propitiatory offering for the redemption of mankind; and has denied his resurrection and ascension into heaven"; "he also denied his mediation and intercession with the Father." He was charged with too much industry in promulgating his views. causing great numbers to embrace them, "and has at length become the leader of a sect distinguished by his name." He was also charged with meeting with, and countenancing by his presence and conduct, those who had "separated" from Friends. This had reference to many meetings of a large majority of the Society held at various places in 1828. The "testimony" also alleges that he had many times been tenderly admonished and advised, but that he and his friends "prevented the timely exercise of the discipline in his case." It all, without doubt, sounded very formidable to the little company of Friends who formulated and issued the document.

This was a remarkable document in more ways than one. The meeting which issued it assumed an authority in conduct hard now to understand, and asserted as facts mere assumptions, and yet we are bound to believe that, in the main, they thought they were performing God's service.

It must be remembered that the orthodox Friends, in 1829, everywhere operated on the theory that those who considered themselves "sound in doctrine," no matter how few in numbers, were the Society of Friends, in direct descent from the founders of the faith. It was their religious duty to excommunicate all whom they considered unsound, even though those disowned might constitute the overwhelming portion of the meeting. That this was the sincere conviction of the orthodox Friends all through the "separation" period, and also before and after it, is a demonstrable fact of history. There was also a marked disposition to adhere to tradition and to cling to former precedents. If there had ever been a time when Friends had been disowned on account of theological opinions, the practice should be kept up, and practically continued forever.

That there was a considerable amount of precedent for disowning Friends on points of doctrine is undoubtedly true. In the famous New Jersey Chancery trial, Samuel Parsons gave several cases of such disownment.[1] They involved cases in half a dozen monthly meetings, and included charges as follows: Denying the miraculous conception; denying the divinity of Jesus Christ; denying the authenticity of the Scriptures; promulgating the belief that the souls of the wicked would be annihilated.

The orthodox Friends might have done still better, and cited the case of John Bartram,[2] the father of American botany, who was disowned by Darby Monthly Meeting in 1758, for deistical and other unorthodox opinions. It has

---

[1] "Foster's Report," Vol. I, p. 171.

[2] John Bartram, born near Darby, Pa., Third month 23, 1699. Was the earliest native American botanist. He died Ninth month 22, 1777. Bartram traveled extensively in the American colonies in pursuit of his botanical studies and investigations. He established the Bartram Botanical Gardens near the Schuykill River, which are still often visited.

been supposed that Bartram was disowned by Friends for placing the following inscription over his door:

> " 'Tis God alone, Almighty Lord,
> The Holy One by me adored.
> John Bartram, 1770."

As this sentiment is dated twelve years after the disownment,[3] it is evident that it was not the primary cause of the action taken by Darby Monthly Meeting.

During the period of repression in the Society, lasting from about 1700 to 1850, it was not hard to find precedent for disowning members on almost any ground, so that the treatment of Elias Hicks, on account of alleged "unsound" doctrine calls for no complaint on the score of regularity. Disowning members for that cause in one branch of Friends to-day would be practically inconceivable. Its wisdom at any time was doubtful, and, in spite of precedents, the practice was not general.

The main point in this transaction, however, is that the meeting which issued the "testimony" against Elias Hicks had no jurisdiction in the case. As a matter of fact, he was never a member of the meeting in question, unless it be assumed that 10 per cent. of two monthly meetings can flock by themselves, organize a new meeting, and take over the 90 per cent. without their knowledge or consent.

In the main, we do not care to consider or discuss the points in the "testimony" under consideration. Those who have followed the pages of this book thus far will be able to decide whether the main causes as stated by those who prepared and approved the document were true in fact, and whether they would have constituted a sufficient reason for the action of the Monthly Meeting of Westbury and Jericho, had it possessed any authority in the case.

---

[3] "Memorials of John Bartram and Humphrey Marshall," by William Darlington, 1849, p. 42.

Just what Elias Hicks thought regarding the matter of Society and disciplinary authority in his case, we have documentary evidence. In a private letter he said: "For how can they disown those who never attended their meetings, nor ever had seen the inside of their new-built meeting-houses, and who never acknowledged their little separate societies? Would it not be as rational and consistent with right order for a Presbyterian or a Methodist society to treat with and disown us for not attending their meetings, and not acknowledging their creed?"[4]

There is one point in the "testimony" which cannot so easily or reasonably be ignored. It says that Elias Hicks "has at length become the leader of a sect, distinguished by his name, yet unjustly assuming the character of Friends." From the assumed standpoint of those who made this statement of fact, it had no warrant. That body of Friends in, at least, the Yearly Meetings of New York, Philadelphia, and Baltimore, which at the time of the "separation" housed two-thirds of all the members, was as much entitled to be called Friends, and assume their "character," as the minority. The distinguishing epithet was not of their selecting or adoption, and those who applied it could scarcely with propriety force it upon those who did not claim it or want it. As for leadership, the outcome in 1827-28 was accomplished without either the presence or assistance of Elias Hicks in a majority of cases. If those who left the parent meetings and set up meetings of their own were the "separatists," then, in a majority of cases, the name belonged to the party that opposed Elias Hicks, and not to that body of Friends who objected to the Society being divided or perpetuated because of the personality or the preaching of any one man.

It has to be said that the disowning at the time of the "separation" was not all on one side. Jericho Monthly

[4] Letter to Johnson Legg, Twelfth month 15, 1829.

Meeting "testified against" at least four of the orthodox party. But in every such case, so far as we are aware, no charges regarding doctrine were made against any. The disownments took place because the persons involved had become connected with other meetings, and did not attend the gatherings of that branch of Friends who issued disownments. Both sides undoubtedly did many things at the time which later would have been impossible.

Elias Hicks evidently approved the general order of the Society in his time touching disownments. In a letter directed to "My Unknown Friend," but having no date, he deals with the disownment question. He goes on to say that it had been the practice of the Society to disown members for more than a century, when such members had deviated "from the established order of Society," and he reaches the conclusion that not to follow this course would lead to "confusion and anarchy." He then says: "These things considered, it appears to me the most rational and prudent, when a particular member of any society dissents in some particular tenet from the rest of that society, if such dissent break communion and render it necessary in the judgment of such society that a separation take place between them, that it be done in the same way, and agreeable to the general practice of such society in like cases."

It is quite certain, however, that Elias Hicks did not think that disputed points of doctrine offered a sufficient ground for disownment in the Society of Friends. In a letter to David Evans, written at Jericho, Twelfth month 25, 1829, he says: "I apprehend that if the Friends who took part in the controversy on the side of the miraculous conception, and those on the opposition, will fully examine both sides of the question, they will find themselves more or less in error, as neither can produce sufficient evidence to enforce a rational conviction on others. . . . Surely, then, we who believe in the miraculous conception ought not to censure our brethren in profession for having a different opinion from ours, and especially as we have no knowledge of the subject in any wise, but from history and tradition. Surely, then, both parties are very far off the true Christian foundation for keeping up the controversy, inasmuch as it never has had the least tendency to gather on the one hand or the other, but always to scatter and divide, and still has the same baneful tendency."

The reader will not fail to consider that at this late period Elias Hicks reiterates his personal belief in the miraculous conception, although the "testimony" of disownment against him charged that he was "endeavoring to destroy a belief in that doctrine." Whatever may have been his belief regarding the latter, it is clear that he did not consider acceptance or rejection of the doctrine a determining quality in maintaining a really Christian fellowship.

CHAPTER XXII.

After the "Separation."

A LETTER dated Solebury, Pa., Sixth month 21, 1828, told of some experiences on his last western trip. It was addressed to his son-in-law, Valentine Hicks. On the journey from Jericho to New York, Elias was very much annoyed, if not vexed, by the crowds of "vain and foolish people coming from the city and its suburbs to see horses trot." "How ridiculous and insignificant," he says, "is such foolish conduct for professed rational beings! I can scarcely conceive in thought an epithet degrading enough to give a just estimate of such irrational conduct."

The "separation" had just been accomplished in the New York Yearly Meeting, and as this was the first visit he had made to the local meetings and Friendly neighborhoods since that event, it is a matter of interest to learn from his own hand how he was received by Friends in the meetings. Rose and Hester Street Meetings, in New York, were attended the First-day after leaving home. Elias says, in the letter mentioned: "They were both large, solemn meetings, showing evidently the comfort and benefit Friends have derived from the orthodox troubles, (they) having separated themselves from us." This may have been the superficial view of many who were prominent in sustaining Elias Hicks. They failed to see, as did their opponents, that the "separation" no matter which side went off, was a violation of the real spirit of Quakerism. It was an unfortunate acknowledgment that "unity of the spirit" was a failure, if it required absolute uniformity of doctrine for its maintenance.

Passing over to New Jersey, he reports universal kindly treatment. In this particular he remarks:

"Indeed we have found nothing in the least degree to discourage or impede our progress, unless it be an excess of kindness from our friends, who can hardly give us up to pass on, without favoring them with a visit in their own houses. And not only Friends, but many who are not members manifest much friendly regard and respect. On Fourth-day we attended Friends' Monthly Meeting for Rahway and Plainfield held at Plainfield, Friends having given their neighbors notice of our intention to be there, it was largely attended by those of other professions, and some of the orthodox Friends, contrary to the expectation of Friends also attended. It was truly a very solemn and instructive good meeting, in which truth reigned. I was truly comforted in the meeting for discipline in viewing Friends' order, and the unity and harmony that prevailed, and the brotherly condescension that was manifested in transacting their business."

Elias Hicks evidently possessed what might be called a grain of humor. In Eleventh month, 1828, when practically all of the "separations" had been accomplished, he wrote to his wife from Redstone, Pa. He had not been getting letters from home as he desired, and especially was that true regarding the much-valued missives from Jemima. He, therefore, says, toward the end of this particular epistle: "If I do not receive some direct account from home at one or both of these places (Alexandria or Baltimore), I shall be ready to conclude that my friends have forgotten me or turned orthodox."

Evidently there had been a readjustment of society conditions in this neighborhood. He says: "Divers friends, whose names I have forgotten, and some who have never seen thee, but love thee on my account, desired to be affectionately remembered to thee. Indeed, love and harmony so abound among Friends in these parts, and the more they are persecuted, the more love abounds, insomuch that I have observed to them in some places, that if they continued faithful to the openings of truth on the mind, that they would so exalt the standard of love and light, that the old adage would be renewed, 'See how the Quakers love one another.'"

Returning from the long western trip, considered in Chapter VI, Elias was met in New York by his wife and daughter Elizabeth, where Westbury Quarterly Meeting was attended. Many near and dear Friends greeted the aged minister, inwardly, if not outwardly, congratulating him upon his safe return home, and the labors so faithfully performed. In mentioning the event, Elias says: "It was truly a season of mutual rejoicing, and my spirit was deeply humbled under a thankful sense of the Lord's preserving power and adorable mercy, in carrying me through and over all opposition, both within and without. He caused all to work together for good, and the promotion of his own glorious cause of truth and righteousness in the earth, and landed me safe in the bosom of my dear family and friends at home, and clothed my spirit with the reward of sweet peace for all my labor and travail. Praises, everlasting high praises be ascribed unto our God, for his mercy endureth forever." [1]

Dark days were approaching, and the heavy hand of a great sorrow was about to be laid upon this strong man, who had buffeted many storms, and who seemed now to be feeling a period of calm and quiet. But we shall let Elias Hicks tell the details in his own words:

"Soon after my return from the aforesaid journey, I had to experience a very severe trial and affliction in the removal of my dearly beloved wife. She was taken down with a cold, and although, for a number of days, we had no anticipation of danger from her complaint, yet about five days after she was taken, the disorder appeared to settle on her lungs, and it brought on an inflammation which terminated in a dissolution of her precious life, on the ninth day from the time she was taken ill. She had but little bodily pain, yet as she became weaker, she suffered from shortness of breathing; but before her close, she became perfectly tranquil and easy, and passed away like a lamb, as though entering into a sweet sleep, without sign or groan, or the least bodily pain, on the 17th of Third month, 1829: And her precious spirit, I trust and believe, has landed safely on the angelic shore, 'where the wicked cease from troubling, and the weary are at rest.' To myself, to whom she was a truly affectionate wife, and to our children, whom she endeavored, by precept and example, to train up in the paths of virtue, and to guard and keep out of harm's way, her removal is a great and irreparable loss: and nothing is left to us in that behalf, but a confident belief and an unshaken hope, that our great loss is her still greater gain; and although the loss and trial, as to all my external blessings, are the greatest I have ever met with, or ever expect to have to endure, yet I have a hope, that, though separated, I may be preserved from mourning or complaining; and that I may continually keep in view the unmerited favour dispensed to us, by being preserved together fifty-eight years in one unbroken bond of endeared affection, which seemed if possible to increase with time to the last moment of her life; and which neither time nor distance can lessen or dissolve; but in the spiritual relation I trust it will endure for ever, where all the Lord's redeemed children are one in him, who is God over all, in all, and through all, blessed forever. She was buried on the 19th, and on this solemn occasion, the Lord, who is strength in weakness, enabled me to bear a public and, I trust, a profitable testimony to the virtues and excellences of her long and consistent life." [2]

Regarding the funeral of Jemima Hicks, and its after-math, rumor has been more or less busy. That Elias spoke on this occasion is certain. It was his eighty-first birthday. His remarks were undoubtedly in harmony, both as to the matter and the hope of a future reunion, with the extract

[2] "Journal," p 425.

printed above. There is in existence what purports to be matter copied from a Poughkeepsie newspaper relating to this event. The statement is supplemented by a "poem," entitled "Orthodox Reflections on the Remarks Made by Elias Hicks at His Wife's Funeral." These verses are both theological and savage. Elias is assured that, because of his belief, he cannot hope to "rest in heaven," or meet his wife there. What is strange, however, is that verses, signed "Elias Hicks," and in reply to the poetical attack, are also given. The first-mentioned rhyme may be genuine, as it voices an opinionated brutality and boldness which was not uncommon in dealing with the future life eighty years ago. But we can hardly imagine Elias Hicks being a "rhymster" under any sort of provocation. If the two "poems" were ever printed, touching the matter in question, some one besides Elias, undoubtedly is responsible for the rejoinder.

Near the 1st of Sixth month, and a little more than three months after the death of his wife, Elias Hicks started on his last religious visit. His concern took him to the meetings and neighborhoods within the limits of his own Yearly Meeting. Nothing unusual is reported on this visit until Dutchess County was reached. All of the meetings were reported satisfactory. Of the meetings at West Branch, Creek and Crum-Elbow, Elias says:

"Although it was in the midst of harvest, such was the excitement produced amongst the people by the opposition made by those of our members who had gone off from us, and set up separate meetings, that the people at large, of other societies flocked to those meetings in such numbers, that our meeting-houses were seldom large enough to contain the assembled multitude; and we had abundant cause for thanksgiving and gratitude to the blessed Author of all our mercies, in condescending to manifest his holy presence, and causing it so to preside as to produce a general solemnity, tendering and contriting

many minds, and comforting and rejoicing the upright in
heart."[3]

Proceeding up the Hudson, arriving at Albany on
Seventh-day, Eighth month 1st, that evening a large meeting was held in the statehouse. Those present represented
the inhabitants generally of the capital city. Many meetings were attended after leaving Albany, which have now
ceased to exist. In fact, few, if any, meetings then in
existence were missed on this journey. The 17th of Eighth
month he was in Utica. Of the meeting in that city, and
at Bridgewater, he says:

"These were not so large as in some other places,
neither was there as much openness to receive our testimony as had generally been the case elsewhere. Our
opposing Friends had filled their heads with so many
strange reports, to which they had given credit without
examination, by which their minds were so strongly preju-
diced against me, that many in the compass of these two
last meetings were not willing to see me, nor hear any
reasons given to show them their mistakes, and that the
reports they had heard were altogether unfounded: however, I was favored to communicate the truth to those who
attended, so that they generally went away fully satisfied,
and I left them with peace of mind."[4]

In 1829, under date of Seventh month 9th, in a letter
written at Oblong, in Westchester County, New York, he
expresses the feeling that the meeting at Jericho sustains
important relations to the branch of Friends with which he
was connected. The letter was written to his children,
Valentine and Abigail Hicks. In it he says:

Although absent in body, yet my mind pretty often
takes a sudden and instantaneous excursion to Jericho,
clothed with a desire that we who constitute that monthly
meeting, may keep our eye so single, to the sure and im-

---

[3] "Journal," p. 428.

[4] "Journal," p. 430.

movable foundation of the light within, so as to be entirely preserved from all fleshly reasonings, which if given way to, in the least degree, ever has, and ever will, have a tendency to divide in Jacob and scatter in Israel. I consider that much depends upon the course we take in our monthly meeting, as we are much looked up to as an example and if we make but a small miss, it may do much harm."

Twelfth month 15, 1829, Elias Hicks wrote to his friend Johnson Legg, evidently in reply to one asking advice in regard to his own conduct in relation to the "separation." In this letter Elias says: "In the present interrupted and disturbed state of our once peaceful and favoured Society, it requires great deliberation and humble waiting on the Lord for counsel before we move forward on the right hand or the left. Had this been the case with our brethren of this yearly meeting who style themselves orthodox, I very much doubt if there would have been any separation among us. For although the chief cause thereof is placed to my account, yet I am confident I have given no just cause for it."

This statement undoubtedly expresses the real feeling of Elias Hicks regarding the "separation." He could not see why what he repeatedly called "mere opinions" should cause a rupture in the Society. It will be noted that he still refers to the other Friends as "our brethren," and he, apparently, had no ill-will toward them. The letter from which this extract was taken was written only about two months before his death, and was undoubtedly his last written word on the unfortunate controversy, and the trouble that grew out of it.

26

CHAPTER XXIII

Friendly and Unfriendly Critics.

FEW men in their day were more talked about than Elias Hicks. The interest in his person and in his preaching continued for years after his death. While the discussion ceased to be warm long years ago, his name is one which men of so-called liberal thought still love to conjure with, without very clearly knowing the reason why. Some clearer light may be thrown upon his life, labor and character by a brief review of opinions of those who criticised him as friends, and some of them as partisans, and those who were his open enemies, for the theological atmosphere had not yet appeared in which he could be even approximately understood by the men of the old school.

We shall begin the collection of criticisms by quoting Edward Hicks,[1] who wrote a comparatively judicial estimate of his friend and kinsman. After stating that even the apostles had their weak side, that Tertullian "was led into a foolish extreme by the fanatical notions of Montanus;" and that Origen "did immense mischief to the cause of primitive Christianity by his extreme attachment

---

[1] Edward Hicks, a relative of Elias Hicks, was born in Attleboro, Pa., Fourth month 4, 1780. His mother passed away when he was an infant, and he was cared for in his early youth by Elizabeth Twining, a friend of his mother. When a young man, he became a member of Middletown Monthly Meeting in Bucks County by request. He began speaking in meeting when about thirty years of age, and was a little later recorded as a minister. Edward Hicks for many years carried on the business of carriage maker and painter at Newtown, Pa. Although much more orthodox in doctrine than his celebrated kinsman, he was one of the most ardent friends and defenders of Elias Hicks.

to the Platonic philosophy, scholastic divinity and human learning," he remarks:

"Therefore, it is among the possible circumstances that dear Elias was led to an extreme in the Unitarian speculation, while opposing the Trinitarian, then increasing among Friends, and now almost established among our orthodox Friends. But I have no recollection of ever hearing him in public testimony, and I have heard him much, when his speculative views or manner of speaking, destroyed the savour of life that attended his ministry, or gave me any uneasiness. But I have certainly heard to my sorrow, too many of his superficial admirers that have tried to copy after him, pretending to wear his crown, without knowing anything of his cross, make use of the naked term, Jesus, both in public and private, till it sounded in my ears as unpleasant, as if coming from the tongue of the profane swearer; and on the other hand, I have been pained to hear the unnecessary repetition of the terms, our Lord and Saviour Jesus Christ, from those I verily believed Elias's bitter enemies, especially the English preachers, and have scarcely a doubt that they were substantially breaking the third commandment. And I will now add my opinion fearlessly, that Elias was wrong in entering into that quibbling controversy with those weak Quakers, alluded to in his letter, about the marvellous conception and parentage of Christ, a delicate and inexplicable subject, that seems to have escaped the particular attention of what we call the darker ages, to disgrace the highest professors of the nineteenth century." [2]

An independent, and in the main, a judicial critic of Quakers and Quakerism is Frederick Storrs Turner, an Englishman. Some of his estimates and observations of Elias Hicks, are both apt and discriminating. Of his preaching Turner says:

"His great theme was the light within; his one aim to promote a true living spiritual, practical Christianity. He was more dogmatic and controversial than Woolman. There seems to have been in him a revival of the old ag-

[2] "Memoirs of Life and Religious Labors of Edward Hicks," p. 92.

gressive zeal, and something of the acerbity of the early Quakers. 'Hireling priests' were as offensive in his eyes as in those of George Fox. He would have no compromise with the religions of the world, and denounced all new-fangled methods and arrangements for religious work and worship in the will of man. He was a Quaker to the back-bone, and stood out manfully for the 'ancient simplicity.'" [3]

With still deeper insight Turner continues his analysis:

"This was his dying testimony: 'The cross of Christ is the perfect law of God, written in the heart . . . there is but one Lord, one faith, and but one baptism. . . . No rational being can be a real Christian and true disciple of Christ until he comes to know all these things verified in his own experience.' He was a good man, a true Christian, and a Quaker of the Quakers. His very errors were the errors of a Quaker, and since the generation of the personal disciples of George Fox it would be difficult to point out any man who had a simpler and firmer faith in the central truth of Quakerism than Elias Hicks." [4]

Regarding some of the bitter criticisms uttered against Elias Hicks at the time of the controversy in the second decade of the nineteenth century, and repeated by the biographers and advocates of some of his opponents, Turner says:

"This concensus of condemnation by such excellent Christian men would blast Hicks's character effectually, were it not for the remembrance that we have heard these shrieks of pious horror before. Just so did Faldo and Baxter, Owen and Bunyan, unite in anathematizing George Fox and the first Quakers. Turning from these invectives of theological opponents to Hicks's own writings, we at once discover that this arch-heretic was a simple, humble-minded, earnest Quaker of the old school." [5]

---

[3] "The Quakers;" a study, historical and critical, by Frederick Storrs Turner, 1889, p. 292.

[4] The same, p. 293.

[5] The same, p. 291.

James Mott, Sr., of Mamaroneck, N. Y., was among
the friendly, although judicial critics of Elias Hicks. In
a letter written Eighth month 5, 1805, to Elias, he said:
"I am satisfied that the Master hath conferred on thee a
precious gift in the ministry, and I have often sat with
peculiar satisfaction in hearing thee exercise it." He then
continues, referring to a special occasion:

"But when thou came to touch on predestination, and
some other erroneous doctrines, I thought a little zeal was
suffered to take place, that led into much censoriousness,
and that expressed in harsh expressions, not only against
the doctrines, but those who had embraced them. . . . I
have often thought if ministers, when treating on doctrinal
points, or our belief, were to hold up our principles fully
and clearly, and particularly our fundamental principle
of the light within, what it was, and how it operates, there
would very seldom be occasion for declamation against
other tenets, however opposite to our own; nor never
against those who have through education or some other
medium embraced them."

This would seem to be as good advice at the beginning of the twentieth century as it was in the first years
of the nineteenth.

In the matter of estimating Elias Hicks, Walt Whitman indulged in the following criticism, supplementing an
estimate of his preaching. Dealing with some opinions of
the contemporaries of Elias Hicks, he says:

"They think Elias Hicks had a large element of personal ambition, the pride of leadership, of establishing perhaps a sect that should reflect his own name, and to which
he should give special form and character. Very likely,
such indeed seems the means all through progress and
civilization, by which strong men and strong convictions
achieve anything definite. But the basic foundation of
Elias was undoubtedly genuine religious fervor. He was
like an old Hebrew prophet. He had the spirit of one, and
in his later years looked like one."[6]

_____

[6] "The Complete Works of Walt Whitman," Vol. 3, p. 269-270.

It is not worth while to deny that Elias Hicks was ambitious, and desired to secure results in his labor. But those who carefully go over his recorded words will find little to warrant the literal conclusion of his critics in this particular. He probably had no idea at any time of founding a sect, or perpetuating his name attached to a fragment of the Society of Friends, either large or small. He believed that he preached the truth; he wanted men to embrace it, as it met the divine witness in their own souls, and not otherwise.

Among the severe critics of Elias Hicks is William Tallack, who in his book "Thomas Shillitoe," says that "many of Elias Hick's assertions are too blasphemous for quotation," while W. Hodgson, refers to the "filth" of the sentiments of Elias Hicks. But both these Friends use words rather loosely. Both must employ their epithets entirely in a theological, and not a moral sense. Having gone over a large amount of the published and private utterances of the Jericho preacher, we have failed to find in them even an impure suggestion. The bitterness of their attacks, simply illustrates the bad spirit in which theological discussion is generally conducted.

The fame of Elias Hicks as a liberalizing influence in religion seems to have reached the Orient. Under date, "Calcutta, June 29, 1827," the celebrated East Indian, Rammohun Roy,[7] addressed an appreciative letter to him. It was sent by a Philadelphian, J. H. Foster, of the ship Georgian, and contained the following expressions:

"My object in intruding on your time is to express the

---

[7] Rammohun Roy was born in Bengal in 1772, being a high-class Brahmin. He was highly educated, and at one time in the employ of the English Government. In comparatively early life he became a religious and social reformer, and incurred the enmity of his family. He published various works in different languages, including English. In 1828 he founded a liberal religious association which grew into the Brahmo Somaj. Roy visited England in 1831, and died there in 1833.

gratification I have felt in reading the sermons you preached at different meetings, and which have since been published by your friends in America. . . . Every sentence found there seems to have proceeded not only from your lips, but from your heart. The true spirit of Christian charity and belief flows from thee and cannot fall short of making some impression on every heart which is susceptible of it. I hope and pray God may reward you for your pious life and benevolent exertion, and remain with the highest reverence.

"Your most humble servant,

"RAMMOHUN ROY."

A copy of what purports to be a reply to this letter is in existence, and is probably genuine, as the language is in accordance with the well-known ideas of Elias Hicks. Besides, an undated personal letter contains a direct reference to the East Indian correspondence. From it we quote: "I take my pen to commune with thee in this way on divers accounts, and first in regard to a letter I have recently received from Calcutta, subscribed by Rammohun Roy, author of a book entitled, 'The Precepts of Jesus, a Guide to Peace and Happiness.' " [8]

A request is made that William Wharton will find out if the ship-master, Foster, mentioned above, would convey a letter to Calcutta. Then Elias expresses himself as follows:

"I also feel a lively interest in whatever relates to the welfare and progress of that enlightened and worthy Hindoo, believing that if he humbly attends to that which begun a good work in him, and is faithful to its manifestations that he will not only witness the blessed effects of it, in his own preservation and salvation, but will be made an instrument in the divine hand of much good to his own people, and nation, by spreading the truth, and opening the right way of salvation among them, which may no doubt prove a great and singular blessing not only to the present, but to succeeding generations. And also be a means of open-

<hr />

[8] From letter written to William Wharton of Philadelphia.

ing the blind eyes of formal traditional Christians, who make a profession of godliness, but deny the power thereof, especially those blind guides, mere man-made ministers, and self-styled missionaries, sent out by Bible and missionary societies of man's constituting, under the pretence of converting those, who in the pride of their hearts they call Heathen, to Christianity, while at the same time, judging them by their fruits they themselves, or most of them, stand in as great, or greater need, of right conversion."

Among the present-day critics of Elias Hicks, is Dr. J. Rendell Harris, of England. In his paper at the Manchester Conference in 1895, this quotation from Elias Hicks is given: "God never made any distinction in the manifestation of his love to his rational creatures. He has placed every son and daughter of Adam on the same ground and in the same condition that our first parents were in. For every child must come clean out of the hands of God." [9] Doctor Harris says Elias Hicks "was wrong not simply because he was unscriptural, but because he was unscientific." [10] Doctor Harris prefaces this remark by the following comment on the quotation from Elias Hicks: "Now suppose such a doctrine to be propounded in this conference would not the proper answer, the answer of any modern thinker, be (1) that we never had any first parents; (2) we were demonstrably not born good." [11] We do not at all assume that Elias Hicks had no limitations, or that he was correct at all points in his thinking, measured by the standards of present-day knowledge or any other standard. But we must claim that in holding that we had first parents, he

---

[9] "Report of the Proceedings of the Conference of Members of the Society of Friends, held by Direction of the Yearly Meeting in Manchester," 1895. p. 220.

[10] The same, p. 220.

[11] We do not hesitate to say that had Elias Hicks made this statement he would have suffered more at the hands of the Philadelphia Elders in 1822 than is recorded in this book.

was scriptural. The poor man, however, seems to have been, unconsciously, of course, between two stools. The orthodox Friends in the early part of the nineteenth century claimed that Elias was unsound because he did not cling to the letter of the scripture, and his critic just quoted claims that he was unscientific although he used a scriptural term. Doctor Harris then concludes that "a little knowledge of evolution would have saved him (Hicks) all that false doctrine." But how, in his time, could he have had any knowledge of evolution? A man can hardly be criticised for not possessing knowledge absolutely unavailable in his day and generation. We are then informed "that the world at any given instant, shows almost every stage of evolution of life, from the amœba to the man, and from the cannibal to the saint. Shall we say that the love of God is equally manifested in all these?" [12] To use the Yankee answer by asking another question, may we inquire, in all seriousness, who is qualified to say with certainty that it is not so manifested? Who has the authority, in the language of Whittier, to

> . . . "fix with metes and bounds
> The love and power of God?"

Elias Hicks was given to using figures of speech and scriptural illustrations in a broad sense, and those who carefully read his utterances will have no trouble in seeing in the quotation used by Doctor Harris simply an attempt to repudiate the attribute of favoritism on the part of the Heavenly Father toward any of his human children, and not to formulate a new philosophy of life, based on a theory of the universe about which he had never heard.

The special labor of Elias Hicks, as we may now dispassionately review it, was not as an expounder of doctrine,

---

[12] Report Manchester Conference, pp. 220-221.

or the creator of a new dogmatism, but as a rationalizing, liberalizing influence in the field of religion. He was a pioneer of the "modern thinkers" of whom Doctor Harris speaks, and did much, amid misunderstanding and the traducing of men, to prepare the way for the broader intellectual and spiritual liberty we now enjoy.

CHAPTER XXIV.

Recollections, Reminiscences and Testimonies.

MANY statements which have come down to us from the generation in which Elias Hicks lived, warrant the conclusion that he was a natural orator. He possessed in a large degree what the late Bishop Simpson, of the Methodist Episcopal Church, called "heart power." We are able to give the personal impression of a venerable Friend[1] now living, who as a boy of eleven heard Elias preach twice.

One of the sermons was delivered at Center, Del., on the 8th of Twelfth month, 1828, and the other the day before at West Chester. This was on his last long religious visit, which took him to the then "far west," Ohio and Indiana.

Doctor Green says that the manner of Elias Hicks when speaking was very impressive. In person he is described by this Friend "as above medium height, rather slim, and with a carriage that would attract universal attention." He wore very plain clothes of a drab color.

With no education in logic, and no disposition to indulge in forensic debate, he was, nevertheless a logician, and had he indulged in public disputation, would have made it interesting if not uncomfortable for his adversary.

If he occasionally became involved, or got into verbal deep water, he always extricated himself, and made his position clear to his hearers. Doctor Green tells us that he had an uncle, not a member of meeting, but a good judge

---

[1] Dr. Jesse C. Green, of West Chester, Pa., now in his 93d year. Doctor Green almost retains the sprightliness of youth.

of public speaking, who considered Elias Hicks the most logical preacher in the Society of Friends. On one occasion he heard Elias when he became very much involved in his speaking, and as this person put it, he thought Elias had "wound himself up," but in a few minutes he came down from his verbal flight, and made every point so clear that he was understood by every listener.

Henry Bryan Binns, Whitman's English biographer, gives the following estimate of the preaching of Elias Hicks:

"With grave emphasis he pronounced his text: 'What is the chief end of man?' and with fiery and eloquent eyes, in a strong, vibrating, and still musical voice, he commenced to deliver his soul-awakening message. The fire of his fervor kindled as he spoke of the purpose of human life; his broad-brim was dashed from his forehead on to one of the seats behind him. With the power of intense conviction his whole presence became an overwhelming persuasion, melting those who sat before him into tears and into one heart of wonder and humility under his high and simple words." [2]

We have another living witness who remembers Elias Hicks. This Friend says that she, with the members of her family, were constant attenders of the Jericho meeting. Speaking of Elias she remarks: "His commanding figure in the gallery is a bright picture I often see in my mind. His person was tall, straight and firm; his manner dignified and noble and agreeable; his voice clear, distinct and penetrating—altogether grand." [3]

We quote the following interesting incidents from the letter of Mary Willis:

"One other bit I recall was a talk, or sermon, to the

---

[2] "A Life of Walt Whitman," Henry Bryan Binns, p. 16.

[3] Extract of letter from Mary Willis, of Rochester, N. Y., dated Ninth month 7, 1910. This Friend is 92 years old. The letter received was entirely written by her, and is a model of legible penmanship and clear statement.

young especially. He related that once he threw a stone and killed a bird, and was struck with consternation and regret at killing an innocent·bird that might be a parent, and its young perish for the need of care. He appealed feelingly to the boys to refrain from giving needless pain.

"He was guardian to my mother, sisters and brother, and they and their mother returned his loving care with warm affection, always, as did my father.

"One of his characteristics was his kindness to the poor. Not far from his home (three miles, perhaps) was a small colony of colored people on poor land, who shared his bounty in cold, wintry weather, in his wagon loads of vegetables and wood, delivered by his own hand."

Probably one of the most appreciative, and in the main discriminative estimates of Elias Hicks, was made by Walt Whitman. The "notes (such as they are) founded on Elias Hicks," for such the author called them, were written in Camden, N. J., in the summer of 1888. Elias Hicks had been dead nearly half a century. Whitman's impressions of the famous preacher were based on the memory of a boy ten years old, for that was Whitman's age when he heard Elias Hicks preach in Brooklyn. But personal memory was supplemented by the statements of his parents, especially his mother, as the preaching of their old Long Island neighbor was undoubtedly a subject of frequent conversation in the Whitman home.

As to the manner of the preacher Whitman says: "While he goes on he falls into the nasality and sing-song tone sometimes heard in such meetings; but in a moment or two, more as if recollecting himself, he breaks off, stops, and resumes in a natural tone. This occurs three or four times during the talk of the evening, till he concludes." [4]

The "unnamable something behind oratory," Whitman says Elias Hicks had, and it "emanated from his very heart to the heart of his audience, or carried with him, or probed

_____

[4] "The Complete Works of Walt Whitman," Vol. 3, p. 259.

into, and shook or aroused in them a sympathetic germ." [5]

There are a good many anecdotes regarding Elias Hicks current in Jericho, going to show some of his characteristics. It is stated that at one time he found that corn was being taken, evidently through the slats of the crib. One night he set a trap in the suspected place. Going to the barn in the morning he saw a man standing near where the trap was set. Elias passed on without seeming to notice the visitor. On returning to the house he stopped, spoke to the man, and released him from the trap. Elias would never tell who the man was.

Illustrating his feeling regarding slavery, and his testimony against slave labor, the following statement is made: Before his death, and following the fatal paralytic stroke, he noticed that the quilt with which he was covered contained cotton. He had lost the power of speech, but he pushed the covering off, thus indicating his displeasure at the presence of an article of comfort which was the product of slave labor.

There is an anecdote which illustrates the spirit of the man in a striking way. He is said to have had a neighbor with whom it did not seem possible to maintain cordial relations. One day Elias saw this neighbor with a big load of hay stalled in a marsh in one of his fields. Without a word of recognition Elias approached the man in the slough and hitching his own ox team to the load in front of the other team proceeded to pull the load out of the slough. It was all done in characteristic Quaker silence. The result was the establishment of cordial relations between the two neighbors.

In bestowing his benefactions, he was exceedingly sensitive, not wishing to be known in the matter, and especially not desiring to receive ordinary expressions of gratitude.

---

[5] The same, p. 264.

His habitual custom was to take his load of wood or provisions, as the case might be, leave them at the door or in the yard of the family in need, and without announcement or comment silently steal away.

During the Revolutionary War, Elias Hicks, in common with other Friends, had property seized in lieu of military service or taxes. The value does not seem to have been great in any of the cases which were reported to the monthly meeting. We copy the following cases from the records:

"On the 28th of Eighth month, 1777, came Justice Maloon, Robert Wilson, Daniel Wilson; and Daniel Weeks, sergeant under the above Captain (Youngs) and took from me a pair of silver buckles, worth 18 shillings; two pair of stockings worth 15 shillings; and two handkerchiefs worth 5 shillings, for my not going at the time of an alarm.—Elias Hicks, Jericho, 24th of Ninth month, 1777." [6]

The "silver buckles" were either for the shoes or the knees. They were evidently more ornamental than useful, and how they comported with the owner's rather severe ideas of plainness is not for us to explain. The price put on these stockings may surprise some twentieth century reader, but it should be remembered that they were long to reach to the knees, and went with short breeches called in the vernacular of the time, "small clothes."

"The 3d of Twelfth month, 1777, there came to my house George Weeks, sergeant under said Captain (Thorne) with a warrant, and demanded twelve shillings of me toward paying some men held to repair the forts near the west end of the island, and upon my refusing to pay, took from me a great coat, worth one pound and six shillings.— Elias Hicks." [7]

We continue the "sufferings," only remarking that the

[6] Westbury Monthly Meeting: "A Record of Marriages, Deaths, Sufferings, etc.," p. 231.

[7] The same, p. 234.

"great coat" was an overcoat, the price at the equivalent of about six dollars and a half was not overdrawn.

"The Sixth month, 1778, taken from Elias Hicks by order of Captain Daniel Youngs, for refusing to pay toward hiring of men to work on fortifications near Brooklyn Ferry, a pair of stockings worth 5 shillings; razor case and two razors, worth 4 shillings." [8]

The next record of "suffering" is more than ordinarily interesting in that it shows that the seizures of property were very arbitrary, and it also gives the price of wheat on Long Island at that time. We quote:

"About the middle of Tenth month, 1779, came George Weeks, by order of Captain Daniel Youngs, and I being from home demanded from my wife three pounds, for not assisting to build a fort at Brooklyn Ferry, for which he took two bags with three bushels of wheat, worth one pound, ten shillings." [9]

At this rate the market price of wheat was $2.50 per bushel. Possibly this was during the period of scarcity, referred to in the introduction.

In 1794 Elias Hicks was influential in establishing in Jericho an organization, the scope of which was described in its preamble as follows: "We, the subscribers, do hereby associate and unite into a Society of Charity for the relief of poor among the black people, more especially for the education of their children." [10]

This society was almost revolutionary at the time of its inception, showing how far-seeing its projectors were. Its constitution declared that the society was rendered nec-

---

[8] The same, p. 242.

[9] The same, p. 254.

[10] This organization has been in continuous existence since its inception. Meets regularly every year, and distributes the proceeds of an Invested fund in accordance with its original purpose.

Friends' Burying Ground, Jericho.   The second head-stone from the right marks the grave of Elias Hicks.

essary because of the injustice and lack of opportunity which the colored people suffered. The hope was expressed that the time would come when the black people would cease to be a submerged and oppressed race. It was provided that in case the original need for the society should disappear, its benefits might be distributed in any helpful way. It may be interesting to note that at the meetings of the society the scarcity of colored children attending the school was mentioned with regret. So far as we know, the Jericho society was the first organized Friendly effort in negro education. Elias Hicks contributed $50 to the invested funds of the organization.

CHAPTER XXV.

Putting Off the Harness.

DURING the series of visits, reported in the twenty-second chapter, Elias was ill a number of times, and was forced to rest from his labors. On the return trip from central and western New York, he visited for the last time the Hudson Valley meetings which he attended on his first religious journey in 1779.

He arrived in New York the 8th of Eleventh month, attending the mid-week meeting at Hester Street that day. On First-day, the 15th, he attended the Rose Street meeting in the morning and Hester Street in the afternoon. Second-day evening, the 16th, a largely attended appointed meeting was held in Brooklyn. He then proceeded toward Jericho, arriving home on Fourth-day, the 18th of Eleventh month, 1829.

The "Journal" is singularly silent regarding this Brooklyn meeting. Henry Byram Binns, on what he considers good authority, says, "Elias Hicks preached in the ball-room of Morrison's Hotel on Brooklyn Heights." To this statement he has added this bit of realistic description:

"The scene was one he (Whitman) never forgot. The finely fitted and fashionable place of dancing, the officers and gay ladies in that mixed and crowded assembly, the lights, the colors and all the associations, both of the faces and of the place, presenting so singular contrast with the plain ancient Friends seated upon the platform, their broad-brims on their heads, their eyes closed; with silence, long continued and becoming oppressive; and most of all, with the tall, prophetic figure that rose at length to break it."[1]

---

[1] "A Life of Walt Whitman," p. 16.

Whitman's own reference to this meeting is still more striking. He says that he, a boy of ten, was allowed to go to the Hicks meeting because he "had been behaving well that day." The "principal dignitaries of the town" attended this meeting, while uniformed officers from the United States Navy Yard graced the gathering with their presence. The text was, "What is the chief end of man?" Whitman says: "I cannot follow the discourse, it presently becomes very fervid and in the midst of its fervor, he takes the broad-brim hat from his head and almost dashing it down with violence on the seat behind, continues with uninterrupted earnestness. Though the differences and disputes of the formal division of the Society of Friends were even then under way, he did not allude to them at all. A pleading, tender, nearly agonizing conviction and magnetic stream of natural eloquence, before which all minds and natures, all emotions, high or low, gentle or simple, yielded entirely without exception, was its cause, method and effect. Many, very many, were in tears." [2]

With the account of this journey of 1829 his narrative in the "Journal" closed. This paragraph formed a fitting benediction:

"The foregoing meetings were times of favor, and as a seal from the hand of our gracious and never-failing helper, to the labor and travail which he has led me into, and enabled me to perform, for the promotion of this great and noble cause of truth and righteousness in the earth, as set forth in the foregoing account, and not suffering any weapon formed against me to prosper. 'This is the heritage of the servants of the Lord, and their righteousness is of me, saith the Lord.' For all these unmerited favors and mercies, in deep humiliation my soul doth magnify the Lord, and return thanksgiving and glory to his great and excellent name; for his mercy endureth forever." [3]

---

[2] "The Complete Writings of Walt Whitman." Issued under the editorial supervision of his Literary Executors, 1902, Vol. 3, p. 258.

[3] "Journal," p. 438.

It should be remembered that Elias Hicks was then past his eighty-first year. He started on this last long religious visit, Sixth month 24th, and was therefore absent from home one week less than five months. He says himself, in the last sentence of the "Journal": "We traveled in this journey nearly fifteen hundred miles." These are words as impressive as they are simple.

During this trip many families were visited from the Valley of the Genesee to the City of New York; where he tarried several days that he might see his friends in their homes. Whatever may have been their mind in the case, he doubtless felt that they would look upon his face no more.

But Elias Hicks was not yet free from his religious concerns, for on First month 21, 1830, he asked for a minute, which was granted by Jericho Monthly Meeting, and is as follows:

"Our beloved Friend, Elias Hicks, presented a concern to make a religious visit to the families of Friends and some Friendly people (as way may open), within the compass of this and Westbury Monthly Meeting, which claimed the solid attention of this meeting, was united with, and he left at liberty to pursue his prospect accordingly."

This is the last minute ever asked for by Elias Hicks. But evidently the visits contemplated were never undertaken, for about that time he had a slight attack of paralysis, which affected his right side and arm. Still the next day he attended a meeting at Bethpage, and a little later quarterly and monthly meetings in New York. In both he performed ministerial service with his usual power and clearness. From a little brochure printed in 1829, we quote:

"In the Monthly Meeting, he took a review of his labors in the city for many years; and then expressed a belief that his religious services were brought nearly to a close.

"After adverting to the great deviations that had taken place in the Society, from that plainness and simplicity into which our principles would lead us, he added, 'but if I should live two or three years longer, what a comfort it would be to me to see a reformation in these respects.' He then spoke in commemoration of the goodness of his Heavenly Father, and closed with these memorable words: 'As certainly as we are engaged to glorify him in all our works, he will as certainly glorify us.'"[4]

But the time of putting off the harness was near at hand. On the 14th of Second month, 1830, he suffered a severe attack of paralysis which involved the entire right side, and deprived him of the use of his voice. When attacked he was alone in his room, but succeeded in getting to his family in an adjoining apartment. He declined all medical aid. In a condition of helplessness he lingered until Seventh-day the 27th, when he quietly passed away. Although he could only communicate by signs, consciousness remained until near the end.

The funeral was held in the meeting house at Jericho, on Fourth-day, Third month 3d. Without a storm raged in strange contrast to the peace and quiet within. A large company braved the elements, to pay their respects to his worth, as a man and a minister, while a number of visiting ministering Friends had sympathetic service at the funeral, after which the burial took place in the ground adjoining the meeting-house, where he had long worshipped and ministered.

The last act performed by Elias Hicks before the fatal stroke came, was to write a letter to his friend Hugh Judge,[5] of Barnesville, Ohio. Between the two men a

---

[4] "Life, Ministry, Last Sickness and Death of Elias Hicks," Philadelphia, J. Richards, printer, 130 North Third Street.

[5] Hugh Judge was born about 1750 of Catholic parents. Joined Friends in his young manhood in Philadelphia. Removed to Ohio in 1815. Died Twelfth month 21, 1834. He died while on a religious

singular sympathy had long existed, and to Hugh, Elias unburdened his spirit in this last word to the world. In fact the letter fell from the hand of the writer, after the shock. It was all complete with signature and postscript.

This letter really summarizes the doctrine, and states the practical religion which inspired the ministry and determined the life and conduct of this worthy Friend. It may be well, with its suggestive postscript, to close this record of the life and labors of Elias Hicks:

"Jericho, Second month 14th, 1830.

"Dear Hugh: Thy very acceptable letter of the 21st ultimo was duly received, and read with interest, tending to excite renewed sympathetic and mutual fellow-feeling; and brought to my remembrance the cheering salutation of the blessed Jesus, our holy and perfect pattern and example, to his disciples, viz: 'Be of good cheer, I have overcome the world.' By which he assured his disciples, that, by walking in the same pathway of self-denial and the cross, which he trod to blessedness, they might also overcome the world; as nothing has ever enabled any rational being, in any age of the world, to overcome the spirit of the world, which lieth in wickedness, but the cross of Christ.

"Some may query, what is the cross of Christ? To these I answer, it is the perfect law of God, written on the tablet of the heart, and in the heart of every rational creature, in such indelible characters that all the power of mortals cannot erase nor obliterate. Neither is there any power or means given or dispensed to the children of men, but this inward law and light, by which the true and saving knowledge of God can be obtained. And by this inward law and light, all will be either justified or condemned, and all be made to know God for themselves, and be left without excuse; agreeably to the prophecy of Jeremiah, and the corroborating testimony of Jesus in his last counsel and command to his disciples, not to depart from Jerusalem until they should receive power from on high; assuring them that they should receive power when they had re-

---

Visit to Friends in Philadelphia Yearly Meeting. Was buried at Kennett Square. He was a recorded minister for many years.

ceived the pouring forth of the spirit upon them, which
would qualify them to bear witness to him in Judea,
Jerusalem, Samaria, and to the uttermost parts of the earth;
which was verified in a marvellous manner on the day of
Pentecost, when thousands were converted to the Christian
faith in one day. By which it is evident that nothing but
this inward light and law, as it is needed and obeyed, ever
did, or ever can make a true and real Christian and child of
God. And until the professors of Christianity agree to lay
aside all their non-essentials in religion, and rally to this
unchangeable foundation and standard of truth, wars and
fightings, confusion and error will prevail, and the angelic
song cannot be heard in our land, that of 'glory to God in
the highest, and on earth peace and good will to men.' But
when all nations are made willing to make this inward law
and light the rule and standard of all their faith and works,
then we shall be brought to know and believe alike, that
there is but one Lord, one faith, and but one baptism; one
God and Father, that is above all, through all, and in all;
and then will all those glorious and consoling prophecies,
recorded in the scriptures of truth, be fulfilled. Isaiah 2:4.
'He,' the Lord, 'shall judge among the nations, and rebuke
many people; and they shall beat their swords into plough-
shares, and their spears into pruning-hooks; nation shall
not lift up sword against nation; neither shall they learn
war any more.' Isaiah 11. 'The wolf also shall dwell with
the lamb, and the leopard shall lie down with the kid; and
the calf, and the young lion, and the fatling together; and
a little child shall lead them. And the cow and the bear
shall feed; their young ones shall lie down together; and
the lion shall eat straw like the ox. And the sucking child
shall play on the hole of the asp, and the weaned child put
his hand on the cockatrice's den. They shall not hurt nor
destroy in all my holy mountain; for the earth,' that is
our earthly tabernacles, 'shall be full of the knowledge of
the Lord, as the waters cover the sea.'

"These scripture testimonies give a true and correct
description of the gospel state, and no rational being can be
a real Christian and true disciple of Christ until he comes
to know all these things verified in his own experience, as
every man and woman has more or less of all those different
animal propensities and passions in their nature; and they
predominate and bear rule, and are the source and fountain
from whence all wars, and every evil work, proceed, and
will continue as long as man remains in his first nature.

and is governed by his animal spirit and propensities, which
constitute the natural man, which Paul tells us, 'receiveth
not the things of the spirit of God, for they are foolish-
ness unto him, neither can he know them, because they are
spiritually discerned.' This corroborates the declaration
of Jesus to Nicodemus, that 'except a man be born again he
cannot see the kingdom of God;' for 'that which is born
of the flesh is flesh, and that which is born of the spirit is
spirit.'

"Here Jesus assures us, beyond all doubt, that nothing
but spirit can either see or enter into the kingdom of God;
and this confirms Paul's doctrine, that 'as many as are led
by the spirit of God are the sons of God, and joint heirs
with Christ.' And Jesus assures us, by his declaration to
his diciples, John 14: 16-17; 'if ye love me keep my com-
mandments; and I will pray the Father and he shall give
you another comforter, that he may abide with you forever,
even the spirit of truth, whom the world cannot receive;'
that is, men and women in their natural state, who have
not given up to be led by this spirit of truth, that leads and
guides into all truth; 'because they see him not, neither do
they know him, but ye know him, for he dwelleth with
you, and shall be in you.' And as these give up to be
wholly led and guided by him, the new birth is brought
forth in them, and they witness the truth of another testimony of Paul's, even that of being 'created anew in Christ
Jesus unto good works,' which God had foreordained that
all his new-born children should walk in them, and thereby
show forth, by their fruits and good works, that they were
truly the children of God, born of his spirit, and taught
of him; agreeably to the testimony of the prophet, that
'the children of the Lord are all taught of the Lord, and in
righteousness they are established, and great is the peace
of his children.' And nothing can make them afraid that
man can do unto them; as saith the prophet in his appeal
to Jehovah: 'Thou wilt keep him in perfect peace, whose
mind is stayed on thee, because he trusteth in thee.' Therefore let every one that loves the truth, for God is truth,
'trust in the Lord forever, for in the Lord Jehovah there
is everlasting strength.'

"I write these things to thee, not as though thou didst
not know them, but as a witness to thy experience, as 'two
are better than one, and a threefold cord is not quickly
broken.'

"I will now draw to a close, with just adding, for thy

encouragement, be of good cheer, for no new thing has
happened to us; for it has ever been the lot of the righteous
to pass through many trials and tribulations in their passage
to that glorious, everlasting peace and happy abode, where
all sorrow and sighing come to an end; the value of which
is above all price, for when we have given all that we have,
and can give, and suffered all that we can suffer, it is still
infinitely below its real value. And if we are favored to
gain an inheritance in that blissful and peaceful abode,
'where the wicked cease from troubling, and the weary are
at rest,' we must ascribe it all to the unmerited mercy and
loving kindness of our Heavenly Father, who remains to
be God over all, blessed forever!

"I will now conclude, and in the fulness of brotherly
love to thee and thine, in which my family unite, subscribe
thy affectionate friend.

"ELIAS HICKS.

"To Hugh Judge:

"Please present my love to all my friends as way
opens."

29

APPENDIX.

A

DESCENDANTS OF ELIAS HICKS.

The only lineal descendants of Elias Hicks are through his daughters, Abigail and Sarah. Abigail's husband, Valentine, was her cousin, and Sarah's husband, Robert Seaman, was a relative on the mother's side.

Descendants of Valentine and Abigail Hicks.

CHILDREN OF THE ABOVE.

GRANDCHILDREN OF ELIAS HICKS.—Caroline, married Dr. William Seaman; Phebe, married Adonijah Underhill (no children); Elias Hicks, married Sarah Hicks; Mary (unmarried).

GREAT-GRANDCHILDREN OF ELIAS HICKS.

CHILDREN OF DR. WILLIAM SEAMAN AND CAROLINE HICKS.—Valentine Hicks Seaman, married Rebecca Cromwell; Sarah Seaman, married Henry B. Cromwell; Samuel Hicks Seaman, married Hannah Husband.

CHILDREN OF ELIAS HICKS AND SARAH HICKS.—Mary, married Peter B. Franklin; Elias Hicks (unmarried), deceased; Caroline (unmarried), deceased.

GREAT-GREAT-GRANDCHILDREN OF ELIAS HICKS.

CHILDREN OF VALENTINE H. AND REBECCA C. SEAMAN.—William, married Addie W. Lobdell; Caroline (infant);[1] Henry B.,[2] married Grace Dutton; Edwin H. (infant); Howard (unmarried), deceased; Valentine H. (unmarried); Emily C. (unmarried); Frederic C., married Ethel Lobdell.

CHILDREN OF HENRY B. AND SARAH SEAMAN CROMWELL.—George[3] (unmarried); Henry B. (unmarried), deceased.

---

[1] NOTE—Those marked "(infant)" died in infancy. Those without notation are under age and living.

[2] Henry B. Seaman is a graduate of Swarthmore College, class of 1881, and received degree of C. E. in 1884. Was for three years Chief Engineer of the Public Service Commission of Greater New York. He resigned this position Tenth month 1, 1910, because he could not approve estimates desired by the authorities. Since then these estimates have been held up as excessive.

[3] When Greater New York was incorporated George Cromwell was

CHILDREN OF SAMUEL H. AND HANNAH H. SEAMAN.—
Joseph H. (unarried); Caroline Hicks, narried William A.
Read; Mary T. (unarried); Franklin (unarried), de-
ceased; Sarah, narried Lloyd Saltus.

CHILDREN OF PETER B. AND MARY HICKS FRANKLIN.—
Anne M., narried Walter A. Campbell.

GREAT-GREAT-GREAT-GRANDCHILDREN OF ELIAS HICKS.

CHILDREN OF WILLIAM AND ADDIE SEAMAN.—Howard
L. (unarried); Jessie M. (unarried).

CHILDREN OF HENRY B. AND GRACE D. SEAMAN.—Ayres
C.; Henry Bowman.

CHILDREN OF FREDERIC C. AND ETHEL L. SEAMAN.—
Esther. . . . .

CHILDREN OF WILLIAM A. AND CAROLINE SEAMAN READ.
—William Augustus; Curtis Seaman; Duncan Hicks; R. Bar-
tow; Caroline Hicks; Bancroft (infant); Bayard W.; Mary
Elizabeth; Kenneth B. (infant).

CHILDREN OF LLOYD AND SARAH SEAMAN SALTUS.—
Mary Seaman; Ethel S.; Seymour; Lloyd.

CHILDREN OF WALTER ALLISON AND ANNE M. FRANK-
LIN CAMPBELL.—Franklin Allison; Mary Elizabeth.

Descendants of Robert Seaman and Sarah, Daughter of Elias Hicks.

CHILDREN OF THE ABOVE.

GRANDCHILDREN OF ELIAS HICKS.—Phebe (died); Hannah, narried Matthew F. Robbins; Willet (died); Elizabeth,
narried Edward Willis; Elias H., narried Phebe Underhill;
Willet H., narried Mary Wing; Mary H., narried Isaac
Willis.

GREAT-GRANDCHILDREN OF ELIAS HICKS.

CHILDREN OF HANNAH AND MATTHEW F. ROBBINS.—
Caroline, narried Sidney W. Jackson; Walter, narried Sarah
E. Hubbs.

CHILDREN OF ELIZABETH AND EDWARD WILLIS.—Sarah
R.; Mary S. (died); Caroline H. (died); Henrietta, narried
Stephen J. Underhill.

CHILDREN OF ELIAS H. AND PHEBE SEAMAN.—Mary
(died); Samuel J., narried Matilda W. Willets; Sarah
(died); Anna; Robert, narried Hannah W. Willets; William

---

elected President of the Borough of Richmond. Although this borough is normally Democratic in its politics, George Cromwell has been
re-elected, and is the only president the borough has ever had. He
and Henry B. Seaman are double first cousins.

H., married Margaret J. Laurie; James H., married (1) Bessie Bridges; (2) Florence Haviland.

CHILDREN OF WILLET H. AND MARY SEAMAN.—Edward W.; Willet H.; Frank W.

CHILDREN OF MARY H. AND ISAAC WILLIS.—Henry, married June Barnes; Robert S.

GREAT-GREAT-GRANDCHILDREN OF ELIAS HICKS.

SON OF CAROLINE AND SIDNEY W. JACKSON.—M. Franklin, married Annie T. Jackson.

CHILDREN OF WALTER AND SARAH E. JACKSON.—Caroline J., married William G. Underhill; Annie H., married Thomas Rushmore; Cora A., married John Marshall.

CHILDREN OF HENRIETTA AND STEPHEN J. UNDERHILL.—Edward W., married Eveline Kissam; Hannah W.; Henry T., married Dorothy Vernon; Arthur.

CHILDREN OF SAMUEL J. AND MATILDA W. SEAMAN.—Mary W., married Leon A. Rushmore; Samuel J., married Ethelena T. Bogart; Anna Louise; Frederick W.; Lewis V. (died).

DAUGHTER OF ROBERT AND HANNAH W. SEAMAN.—Phebe U.

CHILDREN OF WILLIAM H. AND MARGARET L. SEAMAN.—William Laurie; Faith Frances (died).

CHILDREN OF JAMES H. AND BESSIE B. SEAMAN.—George B.; Elias Haviland.

CHILDREN OF JAMES H. AND FLORENCE H. SEAMAN.—Bertha Lucina; Willard H.; Helen U.

GREAT-GREAT-GREAT-GRANDCHILDREN OF ELIAS HICKS.

DAUGHTER OF M. FRANKLIN AND ANNIE T. JACKSON.—Marion F.

CHILDREN OF CAROLINE J. AND WILLIAM G. UNDERHILL.—Mildred; Irene; Margaret.

CHILDREN OF ANNIE H. AND THOMAS RUSHMORE.—Lillian A.; Elizabeth A.

SON OF CORA A. AND JOHN MARSHALL.—John W.

DAUGHTER OF HENRY T. AND DOROTHY UNDERHILL.—Winifred.

SON OF MARY S. AND LEON A. RUSHMORE.—Leon A.

B
Letter to Dr. Atlee.[4]

Copy of a letter from Elias Hicks to Dr. Edwin A. Atlee, of Philadelpia:

"JERICHO, Ninth mo. 27, 1824.

"MY DEAR FRIEND:

"Thy very acceptable letter of the 29th ultimo came duly to hand, and I have taken my pen not only to acknowledge thy kindness, but also to state to thee the unfriendly and unchristian conduct of Anna Braithwaite toward me, not only as relates to that extract, but in her conversation among Friends and others, traducing my religious character, and saying I held and promulgated infidel doctrines, etc.—endeavoring to prejudice the minds of Friends against me, behind my back, in open violation of gospel order. She came to my house, as stated in the extract thou sent me, after the quarterly meeting of ministers and elders at Westbury in First month last. At that meeting was the first time I saw her, which was about five or six months after her arrival in New York. And as I had heard her well spoken of as a minister, I could have had no preconceived opinion of her but what was favorable, therefore, I treated her with all the cordiality and friendship I was capable of. She also, from all outward appearance, manifested the same; and, after dinner, she requested, in company with A. S., a female Friend that was with her, a private opportunity with me. So we withdrew into another room, where we continued in conversation for nearly two hours. And being innocent and ignorant of any cause that I had given, on my part, for the necessity of such an opportunity, I concluded she had nothing more in view than to have a little free conversation on the state of those select meetings.

"But, to my surprise, the first subject she spoke upon, was to call in question a sentiment I had expressed in the meeting aforesaid, which appeared to me to be so plain and simple, that I concluded the weakest member in our society, endued with a rational understanding, would have seen the propriety of. It was a remark I made on the absence of three out of four of the representatives appointed by one of the preparative meetings to attend the quarterly meeting. And I having long been of the opinion, that much weakness had been introduced into our society by injudicious appointments, I

[4] See page 164 of this book.

have often been concerned to caution Friends on that account. The remark I made was this: that I thought there was something wrong in the present instance—for, as we profess to believe in the guidance of the Spirit of Truth as an unerring Spirit, was it not reasonable to expect, especially in a meeting of ministers and elders, that if each Friend attended to their proper gifts, as this Spirit is endued with prescience, that it would be much more likely, under its divine influence, we should be led to appoint such as would attend on particular and necessary occasion, than to appoint those who would not attend?

"This idea, she contended, was not correct; and the sentiments she expressed on this subject really affected me. To think that any, professing to be a gospel minister, called from a distant land to teach others, and to be so deficient in knowledge and experience, in so plain a case, that I could not well help saying to her, that her views were the result of a want of religious experience, and that I believed if she improved her talent faithfully, she would be brought to see better, and acknowledge the correctness of my position. But she replied, she did not want to see better. This manifestation of her self-importance, lowered her character, as a gospel minister, very much in my view; and her subsequent conduct, while she was with us, abundantly corroborated and confirmed this view concerning her. As to her charge against me, in regard to the Scriptures, it is generally incorrect, and some of it false. And it is very extraordinary, that she should manifest so much seeming friendship for me, when present, and in my absence speak against me in such an unbecoming manner. Indeed, her conduct toward me, often reminds me of the treachery of Judas, when he betrayed his Master with a kiss. And, instead of acting toward me as a friend or a Christian, she had been watching for evil.

"As to my asserting that I believe the Scriptures were held in too high estimation by the professors of Christianity in general, I readily admit, as I have asserted it in my public communications for more than forty years, but, generally, in opposition to those that held them to be the only rule of faith and practice; and my views have always been in accordance with our primitive Friends on this point. And at divers times, when in conversation with hireling teachers, (and at other times) I have given it as my opinion, that so long as they held the Scriptures to be the only rule of faith and practice, and by which they justify wars, hireling ministry, predestination, and what they call the ordinances, viz: water baptism and the passover supper, were relics of the Jewish law, so long the Scriptures did such, more harm than good; but that the fault was not in the Scriptures, but in their literal and carnal interpretation of them—and that would always be the case until they came to the Spirit that gave them forth, as no other power could break the seal, and open them rightly to us. Hence I have observed, in my public communications, and in conversation with the members of different denominations, and others, who held that the Scriptures are the primary and only rule of faith and practice—that, according to the true analogy of reasoning, 'that for which a thing is such—the thing itself is more such'—as the Spirit was before the Scriptures, and above them, and without the Spirit they could not have been written or known. And with this simple but conclusive argument, I have convinced divers of the soundness of our doctrine in this respect—that not the Scriptures but the Spirit of Truth, which Jesus commanded his disciples to wait for, as their only rule, they would teach them all things, and guide them into all truth, is the primary and only rule of faith and practice, and is the only means by which our salvation is effected.

"The extract contains so much inconsistency, and is so incorrect, that, as I proceed, it appears less and less worthy of a reply, and yet it does contain some truth. I admit that I did assert, and have long done it, that we cannot believe what we do not understand. This the Scripture affirms, Deut. xxix. 29—'The secret things belong unto the Lord our God, but the things that are revealed belong unto us and our children forever, that we may do all the words of this law'—and all that is not revealed, is to us the same as a nonentity, and will forever remain so, until it is revealed; and that which is revealed, enables us, agreeably to the apostle's exhortation, to give a reason of the hope that is in us, to honest inquirers. I also assert, that we ought to bring all doctrines, whether written or verbal, to the test of the Spirit of Truth in our minds, as the only sure director relative to the things of God; otherwise, why is a manifestation of the Spirit given to every man if it it not to profit by; and, if the Scriptures are about the Spirit, and a more certain test of doctrines, why is the Spirit given, seeing it is useless? But this doctrine, that the Scriptures are the only rule of faith and practice, is a fundamental error, and is manifested to be so by the Scriptures themselves, and also by our primitive Friends' writings. It would seem that Anna Braithwaite has strained every nerve in exaggerating my words, for I have not said more than R. Barclay, and many others of our predecessors, respecting the errors in our English translation of the Bible. Hence it appears, that she was determined to criminate me at all events, by striving to make me erroneous for saying that the Gospel handed to us, was no more authentic than any other writings. Surely a person that did not assent to this, must be ignorant indeed.

"Are not the writings of our primitive Friends as authentic as any book or writing, and especially such as were written so many centuries ago, the originals of which have been lost many hundred years? And are not the histories of passing events, written by candid men of the present age, which thousands know to be true, as authentic as the Bible?

"Her assertions, that I asked if she could be so ignorant as to believe in the account of the creation of the world, and that I had been convinced for the last ten years, that it was only an allegory, and that it had been especially revealed to me at a meeting in Liberty Street about that time; that I asked her if she thought Adam was any worse after he had eaten the forbidden fruit than before, and that I said I did not believe he was; and also her asserting, that I said that Jesus Christ was no more than a prophet, and that I further said, that if she would read the Scriptures attentively she would believe that Jesus was the son of Joseph: these assertions of hers, are all false and unfounded, and must be the result of a feigned or forced construction of something I might have said, to suit her own purpose. For those who do not wish to be satisfied with fair reasoning, there is no end to their cavilling and misrepresentation. As to what she relates as it regards the manner of our coming into the world in our infant state, it is my belief, that we come into the world in the same state of innocence, and endowed with the same propensities and desires that our first parents were, in their primeval state; and this Jesus Christ has established, and must be conclusive in the minds of all true believers; when he took a little child in his arms and blessed him, and said to them around him that except they were converted, and become as that little child, they should in no case enter into the kingdom of heaven. Of course, all the desires and propensities of that little child, and of our first parents in their primeval state, must have been good, as they were all the endowments of their Creator, and given to them for a special purpose. But it is the improper and unlawful indulgence of them that is evil.

"I readily acknowledge, I have not been able to see or understand, how the cruel persecution and crucifixion of Jesus Christ, by the wicked and hard-hearted Jews, should expiate my sins; and never have known anything to effect that for me, but the grace of God, that taught me, agreeably to the apostle's doctrine, to deny all ungodliness and the world's lusts, and do live soberly, righteously, and godly in this present world; and as I have faithfully abode under its teachings, in full obedience thereto, I have been brought to believe that my sins were forgiven, and I permitted to sit under the Lord's teaching, as saith the prophet: 'that the children of the Lord are all taught of the Lord, and in righteousness they are established, and great is the peace of his children.' And so long as I feel this peace, there is nothing in this world that makes me afraid, as it respects my eternal condition. But if any of my friends have received and known benefit from any outward sacrifice, I do not envy them their privilege. But, surely, they would not be willing that I should acknowledge as a truth, that which I have no kind of knowledge of. I am willing to admit, that Divine Mercy is no doubt watching over his rational creation for their good, and may secretly work at times for their preservation; but, if, in his infinite wisdom and goodness, he sees meet to hide it from us, as most consistent with his wisdom and our good, let us have a care that we do not, in the pride of our hearts, undertake to prey into his secret counsels, lest we offend; but be content with what he is pleased to reveal to us, let it be more or less, and, especially, if he is pleased to speak peace to our minds. And when he graciously condescends to do this, we shall know it to be a peace that the world cannot give, with all its enjoyments, neither take away, with all its frowns.

"I shall now draw to a close, and, with the salutation of gospel love, I subscribe myself thy affectionate and sympathizing friend and brother.

"ELIAS HICKS."

To Edwin A. Atlee.

C

The Portraits.

The cut facing page 121 is a photograph from the painting by Henry Ketcham. This was sketched by the artist who was in the public gallery of the meeting house at different times when Elias Hicks was preaching, his presence being unknown to the preacher. It was originally a full-length portrait, but many years ago was injured by fire, when it was cut down to bust size. For some time it was in the home of the late Elwood Walter, of Englewood, N. J. For many years it has been in the family of Henry B. Seaman. It is believed that the pictures made under direction of the late Edward Hopper, had this portrait as their original. The engravings in the "History of Long Island" and in the "Complete Works of Walt Whitman," are probably based on this portrait. They have passed through such a "sleeking-up" process, however, as to lack the individuality of the more crude production.

The frontispiece is from a photograph of the bust of Elias Hicks, by the sculptor, William Ordway Partridge, and was made for Henry B. Seaman. In making the bust the artist used the oil painting referred to above, and all of the other pictures of Elias Hicks in existence, including the full-length silhouette. He also had the bust, said to have been taken from the death mask, and from them all attempted to construct what may be termed the "ideal" Elias Hicks.

D

The Death Mask.

Much has been written about the death mask of Elias Hicks, from which the bust in Swarthmore College, in the New York Friend's Library and other places was made. That such a mask was taken admits of no doubt, and the only clear statement regarding the matter is given below. The bust is in the possession of Harry B. Seaman. The issue of "Niles Register" referred to was published only six weeks after the death of Elias Hicks.

"We understand an Italian artist of this city, has secretly disinterred the body of Elias Hicks, the celebrated Quaker preacher, and moulded his bust. It seems he had applied to the friends of the deceased to take a moulding previous to his interment, but was refused. Suspicion being excited that the grave had been disturbed, it was examined, and some bits of plaster were found adhering to the hair of the deceased. The enthusiastic Italian was visited, and owned that, as he had been denied the privilege of taking a bust before interment, he had adopted the only method of obtaining one. We have heard nothing more on the subject, except that the bust is a most excellent likeness." [1]

---

[1] Quoted from New York Constellation, in "Niles Weekly Register," April 10, 1830, p. 124.

E

A Bit of Advertising.

As showing the way the presence of ministering Friends was advertised in Philadelphia eighty-eight years ago, we reproduce the following, which appeared in some of the papers [1] of that period:

"Arrived in this city on the 7th inst., Elias Hicks, a distinguished minister of the gospel, the Benign Doctrines of which he is a faithful embassador, has for many years past practically endeavored (both by precept and example) to promulgate in its primeval beauty and simplicity, without money and without price. Those who are Friends to plain truth and evangelical preaching, that have heretofore been edified and comforted under his ministry, will doubtless be pleased to learn of his arrival, and avail themselves of the present opportunity of attending such appointments as he, under the direction of Divine influence, may see proper to make in his tour of Gospel Love, to the inhabitants of this city and its vicinity.

"A CITIZEN."

PHILADELPHIA, December 9, 1822.

F

Acknowledgement.

The author of this book acknowledges his indebtedness in its preparation to the following, who either in furnishing data, or otherwise assisted in its preparation: William and Margaret L. Seaman, and Samuel J. Seaman, Glen Cove, N. Y.; Robert and Anna Seaman, Jericho, N. Y.; Henry B. Seaman, Brooklyn, N. Y.; Dr. Jesse H. Green, West Chester, Pa.; Mary Willis, Rochester, N. Y.; Ella K. Barnard and Joseph J. Janney, Baltimore, Md.; Henry B. Hallock, Brooklyn, N. Y.; John Comly, Philadelphia, Pa.

---

[1] The Cabinet, or Works of Darkness Brought to Light. Philadelphia, 1824, p. 33.

G

Sources of Information.

In making this book the following are the main sources of information that have been consulted, which are referred to those who may wish to go into the details of the matter involved:

Journal of Elias Hicks, New York, 1832. Published by Isaac T. Hopper.

The Lundy Family. By William Clinton Armstrong. New Brunswick, 1902.

The Quaker; A Series of Sermons by Members of the Society of Friends, Philadelphia, 1827-28. Published by Marcus T. C. Gould.

A Series of Extemporaneous Discourses, etc., by Elias Hicks. Philadelphia, 1825. Published by Joseph and Edward Parker.

Letters of Elias Hicks. Philadelphia, 1861. Published by T. Ellwood Chapman.

An Account of the Life and Travels of Samuel Bownas. Edited by J. Besse. London, 1756.

Ante-Nicene Fathers. Vol. II. Buffalo, N. Y., 1885. The Christian Literature Publishing Company.

The Quakers. By Frederick Storrs Turner. London, 1889. Swan, Sonnenschein & Co.

A Review of the General and Particular Causes Which Have Produced the Late Disorders in the Yearly Meeting of Friends Held in Philadelphia. By James Cockburn. Philadelphia, 1829.

Foster's Report. Two volumes. By Jeremiah J. Foster, Master and Examiner in Chancery. Philadelphia, 1831.

Rules of Discipline of the Yearly Meeting of Friends Held in Philadelphia. 1806.

The Friend; or Advocate of Truth. Philadelphia, 1828. Published by M. T. C. Gould.

An Apology for the True Christian Divinity, etc. By Robert Barclay. Philadelphia, 1877. Friends' Book Store.

Memoirs of Anna Braithwaite. By her son, J. Bevan Braithwaite. London, 1905. Headley Brothers.

The Christian Inquirer. New York, 1826. Published by B. Bates.

J. Bevan Braithwaite; A Friend of the Nineteenth Century. By His Children. London, 1909. Hodder & Stoughton.

Sermons by Elias Hicks, Ann Jones and Others of the Society of Friends, etc. Brooklyn, 1828.

Journal of Thomas Shillitoe. London, 1839. Harvey & Darton.

Memorials of John Bartram and Humphrey Marshall. By William Darlington, Philadelphia, 1849.

The American Conflict. By Horace Greeley. Hartford, Conn., 1864. O. D. Case & Co.

Memoirs of Life and Religious Labors of Edward Hicks. Philadelphia, 1851.

Life of Walt Whitman. Henry Bryan Binns.

Complete Works of Walt Whitman. 1902.

History of Long Island.

Proceedings of the Manchester Conference. 1895.

Stephen Grellett. By William Guest. Philadelphia, 1833. Henry Longstreth.

ERRATA.

Page 72, 25th line, Elizabeth Hicks died 1871, not 1781.

Page 73, 2d line, Robert Seaman died 1870, not 1860.

Page 74, 7th line, for Martha, read Abigail.

Page 113, next to last line 2d paragraph, for leave, read leaves.

Pages 212, 235 and 242, for Mary Willis, read Sarah L. Willis.

Page 226, to children of Valentine and Abigail Hicks, add Elizabeth.

Page 228, 10th line, for Sarah E. Jackson read Sarah E. Robbins.

INDEX.

238

APPENDIX.

CPSIA information can be obtained
at www.ICGtesting.com
Printed in the USA
BVHW081113211118
533723BV00012B/717/P